JACKIE
STEWART
ON THE
ROAD

JACKIE STEWART
ON THE
ROAD

Illustrations by
David Smith and
John Montgomery

Willow Books
Collins
Grafton Street, London
1983

Willow Books
William Collins & Co Ltd
London Glasgow Sydney Auckland
Toronto Johannesburg

Stewart, Jackie
On the road
1. Automobile driving – Anecdotes, facetiae, satire, etc.
I. Title
796.7'0207   GV1201

ISBN 0 00 218079 0

First published 1983
Copyright © Jackie Stewart 1983

Made by Lennard Books
Mackerye End, Harpenden
Herts AL5 5DR

Editor Michael Leitch
Designed by David Pocknell's Company Ltd
Production Reynolds Clark Associates Ltd
Printed and bound in Spain by
TONSA, San Sebastian

CONTENTS

INTRODUCTION

We were a garage family. My early years in Dumbarton were spent never far from the family garage business, and the sights and sounds of motoring. It was entirely natural that everyone in the family should become a driver, and although I, and my elder brother Jim before me, eventually graduated to motor racing, the most influential motoring figure in my boyhood days was not some oil-spattered Brooklands pioneer, but my mother.

She could not be classified as a Kay Petrie or as one of the suffragettes of motoring, but in our neighbourhood she had a decided reputation as 'the lady in the fast car'. She always drove high-performance cars or cars of peculiar choice. Her enthusiasm for driving was manifest in the parade of extraordinary vehicles which passed through her hands. One that I well recall was a $2\frac{1}{2}$-litre Riley, a bird-like vehicle, dark blue and black with a vinyl roof (very rare in the Forties). In every way the Riley lived up to its image as a *fast* car. Certainly no lady would have been expected to get into such a machine without serious risk to her dignity. Getting in also required a considerable degree of gymnastic skill. Not the least of the Riley's problems was that the front doors opened forward, so if one of them came open on the road, instead of blowing shut, it blew off completely.

It goes without saying that my mother drove that car *fast*. I have since thought that anyone doing research into the genetics of motoring need look no further than Mrs Stewart and her sons. My brother Jim is eight years older than I, so he experienced the impact of my mother's talents behind the wheel long before I did. Later she was to deny vigorously that her driving had any effect on either of us, and she was equally vehement that we should *not* take up racing. But if ever a driving bug was implanted in our minds, it undoubtedly came from her.

My father in his younger days was also fired by the quest for speed, but mostly this was channelled into motorcycles. He was friendly with Graham Walker, father of Murray Walker, the BBC motor-racing commentator. He went to the TT races and did a lot of riding, and his old scrapbooks contain many photographs showing him astride various weird devices that, he assured me, were different species of motorcycle.

In the matter of speed on *four* wheels, however, it was my mother who was the founding influence. It is somewhat strange, looking back, to realize how all-pervading that influence turned out to be. This was in part due to her preference for driving vehicles that were not so much cars as self-contained chapters in the mythology of motoring. As a small boy it was difficult for me not to be enveloped by their spell, even though at times I had my reservations.

One of her cars that excited mixed feelings was an Austin Atlantic convertible. This amazing piece of streamlined chrome-on-wheels was more suited to American tastes than Scottish, and one of its claims to fame indeed was that it was taken to Indianapolis and driven for numberless hours round the US racing circuit to establish new records of endurance. Had the *Guinness Book of Records* been around at the time, this car's efforts would surely have been included.

So much for its performance. There was also the less happy matter of its aura (appearance is not a strong enough word). It looked like the first British Plushmobile – so overdone as to be way beyond anything that any other luxury car could even suggest. Its basic shape was that of a duck, and it would probably have been a simple matter to convert it for amphibious work. It seemed immensely long, and had great stripes of chrome running along the bonnet and the body which was painted powder-blue. To be picked up by it outside the austere stonework of Dumbarton Academy was sometimes a painful embarrassment. None of the other boys' parents had anything remotely so flash. Flashness, moreover, was widely held to be morally suspect, and it was a vain exercise to point out any of the car's advanced design features, such as its electric windows. Electric windows?!!! Flashness in 1950 was permitted *no* redeeming features.

The Austin Atlantic stood, fortunately, at the extreme edge of my mother's taste for spectacular cars. Of the more likeable cars she drove, I remember a TR-2 – the first Triumph sports car to come out – which was followed by a TR-3, which was followed by a Jaguar XK-120. This last was the epitome of all sports cars, in masculine terms the horniest thing you could let your hands be loose on. It was certainly an extraordinary choice for a lady.

From the XK-120 – and for reasons that escape me, unless, as Austin dealers, we had been stuck with it at the garage – my mother progressed to an Austin Metropolitan. This was a squat, dumpy car with half-concealed wheels which, if you ignored its hideous brick-orange-and-white two-tone colouring, could have passed for a small brother of the Plushmobile duck. While it had no performance to speak of, it was a very friendly car: as it went along the road, it nodded to everyone. The suspension was so weak that the car had this curious flopping motion. If in fact it had been a duck, and not a car, it would have been one of those clockwork types that capsize with such readiness in the bath. On the other hand, while it may have been mechanically unexciting, the Metropolitan did have one marvellous piece of equipment, not exactly a recent invention but still quite a rarity – a car radio! (Courting couples also had reason to be grateful for the umbrella handbrake and steering-column gearchange, which gave them more space for their manoeuvres, but that is another story.)

However, even the thrill of hearing music come out of the dashboard could not keep a true motorist quiet for long. When its adoption papers were signed, the Metropolitan moved on to a more suitable home, leaving Mother to console herself with an XK-140 that just happened to come along at the right moment.

Such was the unpredictable atmosphere in which I passed the early years of my life. It prepared me well, not only for my later career in motor racing, but also for the planning and compiling of this book. Like the sequence of cars which my mother elected to drive, this book, deliberately, has no obvious or rigid pattern. It is neither a manual, nor a history, nor an autobiography. I would describe it as an after-hours companion which takes the whole diffuse subject of motoring, delves into its past, speculates on its present nature, and tries to show just what it is that separates the motorist from all other living creatures on this planet. My hope is that motorists throughout the world – whether they live in Brazil, the Bronx, Birmingham or Brisbane – will be able to recognize both themselves and each other. I hope, also, that they like what they see!

THE
UNIVERSAL
MOTORIST

The hazards of driving in another country are such that every motorist should ensure that he or she is baptized in the necessary arts at an early age, before family obligations are assumed and youthful fearlessness is supplanted by the middle-aged nightmare of setting out to explore foreign lands, and ending the expedition in some grisly pile-up: 'Sunseekers in M-way Holocaust'.

The chief problem in coping with foreign motorists, whoever you are, is not so much remembering that they are different from yourself, but that they are enormously variable. Cross a frontier without adjusting to the new vehicular mob, say from Switzerland to Italy, and you can be in deep trouble.

My own teenage memorial to foreign travel is a remarkable mirror system which I fitted before taking an Austin A35 from Scotland to Geneva. The object was for the driver of a right-hand-drive British car to be able to see round the Continental traffic travelling ahead of him on the right-hand side of the road and judge whether it was safe to overtake. So, in additional to the usual rear-view mirror, I had two others inside the car; we'll call them Mirrors A and B. Mirror A was fixed near the normal interior rear-view mirror and was angled across to pick up the reflections appearing in Mirror B, which was sited in the left top corner of the windscreen and turned to look forward up the road and gather information about oncoming traffic. By the time I got to Geneva – driving non-stop from Calais with one co-driver – I was so shattered, and fed up with overtaking by mirrors alone, I wanted to sell the wretched car and travel home by air. Swiss inflexibility over the re-sale of imported motor cars forbade this, however, and I was stuck with the unwelcome machine for many miles to come.

It was on that journey that I learned to be wary of those endless straight country avenues which the French line on both sides with poplar trees – surely one of the most lethal forms of crash barrier ever invented since there is certainly no space to go between the trees if you come off the road at speed. Then there was *priorité à droite*.

In those days *priorité à droite* was nothing less than the divine right of Frenchmen to shoot out of a side turning with no warning and ram whatever lay in their path. This right is exercised less widely today, but curiously enough I survived the *priorité* system for some two decades before being finally caught in Rheims by a kamikaze *camionette* which roared out from the right, somersaulted across my front bumper and turned itself completely over, finishing the move in a mound of fruit and vegetables which rained down from nearby market stalls situated on the outskirts of the action. No-one was hurt, but the possibilities of the havoc that this lunatic regulation could create became firmly imprinted in my mind.

FILTHY HABITS

One of the greatest gulfs separating the driving nations is that untarmacadamed void known as the Atlantic Ocean. More precisely, it is the mental distance between the European and the American motorist, particularly the South American motorist. Compare, for example, an English driver at a set of traffic lights with a Brazilian.

Very rarely will an Englishman try to anticipate the green light by moving off prematurely. You will find the occasional sharpie who watches for the amber to come up on the adjacent set of lights; if he is really tweaked up he has already engaged gear and has the engine revving and the clutch within a hairsbreadth of release. However, he will not *go* until he receives the lawful signal. The only exception to this is the taxi driver who may crawl forward a few yards – usually so he can turn right before the oncoming stream gets started. But as a people the English are not inclined to exert themselves unduly at traffic lights.

Brazilians view the thing quite differently. If in fact they see traffic lights at all, they regard them as a kind of roadside decoration, to be enjoyed for their bright colours, and not at all as an instrument designed to have some bearing on the pace of the vehicle they are currently guiding through a crowded intersection.

Back in Europe, one nation above all others lives scrupulously by its traffic lights: the Swiss. In Switzerland, if you were to anticipate a light the chances are that the motorist behind you would take your number and report you to the police. What is more, the police would visit you; *and* you would be convicted. The Swiss take their rules of the road so seriously that a driver can be summonsed and charged for speeding on hearsay alone, and very likely found guilty. There are slight regional variations among the French, German and Italian speaking areas, but it is generally safe to assume that any car bearing a CH sticker will be driven with a high degree of discipline.

A sense of discipline is not something that just pops into people's heads overnight; it takes many years and more than one generation to become established. That possibly explains why the Belgians are such notoriously bad drivers, for until the 1960s they had no form of driving test at all. Consequently their regard for rules of the road is slight and their accident rate little short of horrendous.

Italians are distinguished by their disrespect for speed limits and preference for flair over civil obedience. This means, for instance, that they may pass you on the outside or the inside; it is the sort of decision that is left to the last moment in case some more aesthetic solution should propose itself, opening the way for a more brilliant or complex swerve. Their manual gestures are of a greater variety and expressiveness than those of any other nation in Europe, and they are the least safety-conscious of peoples, professing a very low opinion of seat belts. They are fluent with the horn, which is regarded as a species of musical instrument and is available in a wondrous range of notes and noises. They play their instruments, moreover, with style and – on the whole – good humour, which marks them off from their slightly less Latin neighbours, the French, who are inclined to use the horn snappishly and to promote their sense of self-righteousness.

Paris, in the period since August 1944 when it was liberated from the Germans, rapidly filled to ear-bursting point with a new generation of apoplectic French motorists. The uproar in the more spacious meeting places, such as the Place de la Concorde, grew so dreadful in the next decade that people began to think the Eiffel Tower had been turned on its side and converted, specifically for their discomfort, into a gigantic municipal ear trumpet. There was confusion on a grand scale. Drivers in a traffic jam no longer knew whether it was best to hoot back, or wind up the windows and cover their ears with both hands, or cover their ears and simultaneously hoot back using an elbow to press the horn; or just scream. Eventually the government had to intervene and the horn was banned in the capital.

The other remarkable feature of the French driver is the amount of alcohol he is prepared to consume before taking the wheel. This has always been so, as far back as horse-drawn days when postilions and drivers were constantly dropping off

to sleep after a heavy session at the last *auberge,* and the safe
arrival of a coach depended greatly on the goodwill and
navigational ability of the horses. Today's archetypal
descendant of the slumbering postilion is a rosy-cheeked
overweight countryman – an expert in some rare rural trade
such as making bungs for wine barrels – weaving home in his
faithful old grey Citroen 2CV after a two-litre
lunch with the mayor and a few friends.

Should the unthinkable happen, and the bureaucrats of Paris decide in a rush of puritanism to introduce breathalyzer squads in rural areas, then an entire centuries-old way of life could be threatened. It would almost certainly have the effect of depopulating the great network of 'D' roads, hitherto the safe preserve of the drinking driver. It would then be interesting to see what happened next. Would the spirit of the Resistance reassert itself, perhaps in the form of American-style off-road vehicles which the crafty drinking driver could use to outwit the police road blocks? Those would be exciting times, and though it is entirely feasible to imagine them happening in France, it is certain they would never do so in neighbouring Germany.

FLASHERS

The Germans drive with a singular blend of aggression and discipline, and it is essential if you wish to keep your skin intact that you understand the rules of the road. On the autobahns a lot of driving behaviour stems from the lack of an ultimate speed limit. You may not, for instance, overtake on the inside; to do so invites an automatic heavy police fine. What, then, do you do if the great hulk of a Mercedes in front of you is being driven at less than top speed and will not move over and let you through? Answer: you give it the flashing light treatment.

The flashing ultra-bright light has no more ideal habitat than the German autobahn. Typically, it is mounted in pairs on a Porsche 911 Turbo or a Mercedes 500 – one of those symbols of pure power which the Germans so dearly love – and it suddenly appears out of nowhere in your rear-view mirror, travelling at around 150 mph. Your first reaction is to wonder if it isn't yet another Starfighter jet crash-landing on the motorway; when you are at last able to make out the vehicle behind the lights, you see it is only an enormous battleship-grey autobahn cruiser being driven by an enormous man smoking an enormous cigar. You have barely had time to move over before he sweeps silently past; one finger remains permanently poised above the firing button of his laser device, and soon enough he is at it again, eating up his next victim a mile down the road.

Moving north, we come to Scandinavian lands, where the motorist lives in perpetual conflict with the law. At the root of his problem is the way he drinks – knocking back the distilled potato in killer bursts that guarantee oblivion in little more than half.an hour. To keep the roads of Sweden, Norway, Finland, etc, even halfway clear of helpless drunks, the authorities have cracked down with some weighty sanctions: at the top of their list is instant jail without the option, followed by massive suspensions and fines requiring a second mortgage to pay off.

The unpleasantness of these thundering punishments has now filtered into the public awareness, and the result is that most Scandinavians try with touching earnestness to separate their driving from their drinking. Thus, at a party, if there are four cars parked outside the house you know that inside there will be four thoroughly sober, thoroughly miserable Swedes. It is impossible from the outside to calculate how many stupefied guests are present since Nordic partygoers have cunningly taken to giving each other lifts, cramming as many as possible into one car and thereby minimizing the number of non-drinking nights any one driver will have to serve in the course of a year.

WILD WEST

Back in the 15th and 16th centuries the Iberian peninsula was a principal jumping-off point for the New World. Spanish and Portuguese adventurers and explorers colonized South America, and you can still discern similarities in the way the peoples of these various countries conduct themselves on the road. Continuing poverty on both sides of the Atlantic has meant that among today's drivers there is still a high proportion of first-generation highway users. They are coming off the farms – out of the jungle, even – to take their chances on busy roads containing large numbers of motorists who are just as wild, and ignorantly confident, as they are. What these drivers also lack – and will never benefit from – is the chance to sit round the family table and talk about their highway experiences, and so build up their knowledge of motoring without having to learn it all the hard way by doing it themselves. Much the same can be said of drivers in many other Third World countries, whether in Africa or the East.

The natives of North America are much more conformist and disciplined. They demonstrate this in their addiction to driving in one lane and sticking to it – even if it means settling behind some great articulated truck for many miles. They would rather be in the fast lane, of course, but this is not necessarily the one on the extreme left. The traffic in the inside lane of a six-lane highway may actually be going faster than all the others. This does not matter. The important thing is not to dive and weave about. To prevent other drivers from falling into flamboyant ways, American motorists try always to stay close behind the vehicle in front – which can make it impossible, when the whole flotilla is moving at about 55 mph, to make a *bona fide* lane change. European visitors are constantly falling into this trap: they return to the Old World still flapping their arms in frustration because while driving in the States in their Hertz car they kept failing to get off the highway when they wanted to and were swept along to the next city.

The natives of New York stay resolutely in the jungle which they have created for themselves and which is quite unlike the rest of the country. Noise and chaos rule in the city, which has now taken over from Paris as the capital of the horn, as drivers inch their way to different points on the implacable grid. (New York seems also to be the world's Research & Development centre for testing any new extreme sound that might be suitable for fitting to emergency vehicles.)

Progress on the city streets is made, as in American football, by a mixture of blocking moves and rushes. Intersections are where most of the action takes place. The first move is to edge over to the centre of the crossing – preferably after the lights have changed – and wedge your vehicle at an angle so that following traffic is blocked. Traffic now attempting to move across the intersection in the opposite direction may also be blocked but that, curiously, does not seem important. The main aim is to establish a position of strength so that, within no more than a dozen changes of lights, you will have excavated a hole wide enough to dash suddenly clear of the pack and be first up to the next intersection, where the entire process is repeated.

Driving in New York is at once highly stimulating and immensely boring. The great rule is that you should not weaken. If you haven't tried it yet, go there soon. Unfortunately, the signs are that the roads of Manhattan Island are about to crack and collapse under the tremendous overload they have borne since the age of the automobile began. In addition to the usual subterranean geysers that spray steam to a height of six feet, and the potholes up to two feet deep which appear overnight, serious fissures measuring several feet across have been opening without warning, capable of swallowing large numbers of autos before the appropriate city authority truck can tunnel a path through the surrounding blocks of jammed and hooting traffic and unload its crew who then cover the crevass with one of the specially pre-rusted reinforced steel plates which have been developed for this very purpose.

On the basis that what happens this year in New York can be expected within a couple of years to spread to cities in other countries and continents, there is a strong case for arguing that the End of the urban motorist is Nigh.

PANTOMIME WITH HORNS

I_f

there can be such a thing as innocent indoctrination,
it is surely the process by which today's child is drawn
in to the world of motoring. Provided his parents have a
car, the rest is inevitable. From the day the child ceases
to take his journeys in a horizontal position, he
becomes a captive back-seat spectator at one of the
world's longest-running comedy shows.

There he sits, strapped in full harness to a
purpose-built contraption almost indistinguishable
from the seats used by Formula One racing drivers.
(The similarity is certainly not lost on any TV-watching
infant of average intelligence.) Meanwhile, up front,
what are his parents doing?

On that particular Saturday morning they
were driving out of town to the hypermarket when,

without warning, the car came to an abrupt halt. The horns that usually sprout from Father's head each time he takes the wheel have suddenly doubled in length, giving him the look of an enraged devil-goat, and both he and the normally restrained lady sitting next to him – the child's Mother – are suddenly unleashing a torrent of unfamiliar words and phrases, accompanied by frenzied blasts on the car-horn.

The child senses his parents' mood accurately enough, but cannot account for it. His previous experience of their anger is limited to what happens when he drops his orange juice on the carpet. This present display is clearly much more dramatic, both in terms of the words used, the venom shown and the noise generated. For the first time, in fact, the child sees his parents doing unto others what, previously, they had done only unto him. What is more, the victims of this violent attack are people of his parents' own size and age. From the cocooning safety of his Formula One shell, he watches and marvels.

It seems, from the way their heads are turned, that his parents' frustration is directed at the occupants of another car which has stopped halfway across their path and is preventing them from moving forward. As they yell the ritual obscenities, the child notices another oddity: the people in the other car seem not to be taking the slightest notice. Could this be, he wonders, because they are shut in their own metal box several feet away and simply cannot hear what his parents wish them to know?

The child is half right. Indeed, the people in the other car cannot hear a word of what is being said. What the child does not yet know is that in some parts of the world it is standard behaviour to ignore anyone who could be so vulgar as to hoot at one. Unless, of course, one is stuck in traffic, in which case one's self-respect requires that some retaliatory action be taken after a suitable interval.

The other driver has now reached the stage of needing to retaliate. He responds by turning his head and jabbing a finger towards the roof of his own car, as though he wants to poke a hole in it, and mouthing a fierce-looking message back at the child's parents who, in turn, cannot hear any of it. Father replies with half a dozen angry blasts on the car-horn. The other driver looks away again, presumably to show that he has not heard the horn, and points this time at his windscreen. Ah, thinks the child, perhaps he is pointing *through* the window at something beyond; possibly at the red traffic light on the other side of the road.

Father begins to shout. 'We know all about that,' he yells, adding 'you stupid bloody idiot! You're blocking our way.' He hits the horn again, giving it one long blast.

The other driver raises his eyebrows, then shrugs his shoulders in slow motion. 'What can I do?' he seems to be saying. 'I can't move until the lights change, can I?' His impotence, and implied guilt, are emphasized by the ashamed reaction of his female companion, who throughout the entire exchange glares away in the opposite direction, her lips tightly pursed; she, it is clear, wants no part of it.

Father notes this but is not placated. He has built up a full head of steam against the other driver, and must release it. 'How could anyone *be* so stupid?' he screams, and jerks his hands up in the air.

'Exactly,' shouts Mother in support. 'Just look at his smug little monkey face, trying to blame it on the traffic lights. What an absolute *idiot!*' She flaps her hands in the air, then slaps them on her thighs.

The other driver has been observing these gestures, and now responds by pulling his features into a hideous grimace, glaring all the while with great round eyes at Father and Mother. The effect is dynamic. War has been declared.

'Right,' yells Father. 'That's it. Cheeky sod! I'm going to put one on him.'

An instant later Father has flung open his door. Mother, alarmed, tries to stop him. She lays a restraining hand on Father's arm. 'No, dear,' she cries. 'I don't think you ought to go quite that far . . .'

As though to reinforce her judgment, Father's seat belt now comes into play and twangs him back into his rightful place. Before he can find the belt catch and struggle loose, the traffic light across the street changes to green; the car standing across their path surges away to safety, its driver bent forward over his wheel, staring intently ahead.

'Damn and blast!' yells Father, still wrestling with his seat belt. 'The little creep's getting away!'

The child in the Formula One seat gazes in astonishment at the vanishing rear of the other car. He is puzzled that his Father should now be sorry to see the other man go, when previously he had been cross with him for getting in the way.

As the child mulls over what he has just seen, his train of thought is brusquely interrupted. The traffic lights have changed once more, and the family car becomes a mad orchestra of clashing gears and squealing tyres, then rockets away from the scene of the incident. The pantomime is over.

Ah, thinks the child when he has recovered breath. That's more like it. Speed! For a little while yet, the politics of the highway will remain something of a grey area in his mind – though doubtless he will get the hang of things one day. On the other hand, speed – the thrill of being towed along at ten times the rate of a runaway pushchair – is something at once intensely special and simple to comprehend. The child's thoughts turn with keen anticipation to the little pedal-powered racer which he keeps in a corner of the family garage, and which it is his delight to drive as fast as possible into oily patches on the floor, then skid and slide as though his life depended on it. One day it very likely will.

Is it any wonder, with his own machine to drive and his parents' to ride in, that motoring, already, has become a full-time obsession?

BOY ON
A PETROL
CAN

I

took my first serious driving lessons at the age of nine in my father's garage. The vehicle was an Austin 16, and the letters in the registration number were BUC. Later I had a go on a TR-2 that was passing through my mother's hands at the time, but my main early practical experience was gained in BUC.

BUC was a large, pre-war, dark blue and black, four-door device. The gear lever was a long gently curving stick that rose out of the floor and terminated in a bakelite knob the size of two golf balls melted together. The steering wheel was also on the large side and made of bakelite, and the dials on the dashboard, though few in number, were sturdily built and easy to read, as solid as nautical clocks. The handbrake was a massive lever with a ratchet, such as you still find in railway signal-boxes.

At that age, understandably, I was even smaller than I am today. As a nine year-old, I must have been approximately the size of an average three year-old. It was therefore necessary to raise me up so that I could peer through the spokes of the steering wheel and get a tolerable view of where I was driving. My auxiliary seat was a square, two-gallon petrol can laid on its side, and from this station I could see out sufficiently well to drive BUC back and forth in the parking area of the garage forecourt and, at a further stage of my development, venture in and out of the petrol pumps, then in through one door of the garage building and out the other.

As I gained confidence, these manoeuvres were carried out at ever-increasing speed – to the consternation of the garage staff and the even greater consternation of visitors and customers who could not easily see the small form behind the wheel of the large Austin bearing down on them; some indeed could not have been certain that it was being driven by anyone at all.

The next development, as I grew cockier, was skid practice. The great thrill of the year came with the arrival of snow and ice. Then I could get up some speed and spin BUC in the forecourt and down a hill just in front of it. Regrettably, there were not many days when the snow was sufficiently hard-packed to have a real thrash on it, but the excitement that came from making BUC perform power-turns in the forecourt was one of the best sensations of my childhood, if not *the* best. The exercise was given added spice by the ever-present risk of side-swiping other cars on the forecourt, and I know my parents viewed this prospect with some gravity. Never once, though, did I let them down by scraping either one of their vehicles or a customer's.

By the time I was twelve I was going up with the garage mechanics to test cars on a nearby private estate at

Overton, and getting in a few quick bursts at the wheel which helped to extend my horizons beyond the garage forecourt. By then my brother Jim had started to drive racing cars. He began with an MG TC, competing in sprints and hill climbs, and I went with him to the meetings, at Turnberry, Boness near Grangemouth, and elsewhere. At these gatherings I sighted my first aces – such giants as Raymond Mays, Ken Wharton, Sid Allard, Dennis Poore and Basil Davenport – and became caught in the whole atmosphere of competitive motoring. I collected autographs and kept a scrapbook into which all kinds of goodies found their way. Another great bonus of having a brother who raced, was being driven at speed. There was then no top limit on the open road, and to see the needle slide past 100 mph in my brother's car – by then a Healy Silverstone – was an intense thrill for someone barely on the fringe of his teens.

Even better was the occasion I myself drove at speed for the first time. The venue was a disused airfield, to which my brother took me; there, at last, I was able to press my foot down in a meaningful way, going right up through the gears and down again. In those non-synchromesh days it was obviously necessary to get one's timing right for such exercises. In my case, with four more years to go before I could have my own licence, the biggest problem was finding enough opportunities for practice.

Bikes presented other ways of learning to control a moving vehicle. At one time in early adolescence I had a moped, given to me by Ninian Sanderson, a well-known Scottish racer, on which I used to tear round a special course marked out with empty oil drums. Throughout these juvenile adventures I cultivated my own personal emblem of speed: a leather cap with earflaps, dimly related to World War I flying helmets and motorcyclists' caps but possessing enough idiosyncratic straps, flaps and extra pieces to be more suggestive of the type of hat Sir Vivian Fuchs would have favoured for climbing Mount Everest.

Looking back on those years, and comparing notes with other drivers, particularly those who became professional racers, the extraordinary thing was to find that they too were up to almost identical tricks, each man adapting to his local terrain, climate and personal background. What is more, as we shall see in the next chapter, these and other strange related habits seem to be attracting a far wider following amongst the young of today.

FIRST KICKS

The name of the game for the under-age enthusiast is: off-road. In the years when young people are bubbling with exuberance but too young to take out a licence, there are a dozen ways to experience the thrills of driving at speed without breaking the law. Among racing drivers, Ronnie Peterson, Emerson Fittipaldi and Ricardo Patrese got their early kicks from racing go-karts. The late Gilles Villeneuve, who grew up in Canada, drove snowmobiles. Others used motorbikes, or farm machines; or had access to some piece of private land where they could race a car down farm roads and over fields, spinning it across the wet grass.

One way or another they learned the rudiments of car control, and at the same time acquired that hideous, paradoxical enthusiasm for doing things that were *out* of control. It is, I believe, a mark of our present cotton-wool society that more and more young people are turning to off-road driving as a means of escaping the wraps put round them by Authority in all its guises, to see what it is like to place their lives exclusively in their own hands.

This urge to go to the outer perimeters of life and experience the closeness of injury or death, to do it often, and feel the adrenalin pumping, is surely one of the reasons why people take up motor racing. Others climb mountains to get away from the shackles of ordinary life and experience the dangers of freedom to the limits of their wishes. To feel that kind of 'high' today, without resorting to drugs, is actually becoming more difficult. The concern for over-protection in our consumer-based society has become a matter of such high priority that, while admirable insofar as it reduces the likelihood of foreseeable accidents, it may also condition future generations to see risk-taking as an undesirable, perhaps anti-social activity. If that ever happens, we shall all be the losers.

Fortunately, many young people today are loudly insisting that they have no desire to knuckle under. They want their kicks, and many see speed as the means. For those who are under-age, the sensible direction to go is off-road. In this first, experimental period two wheels are as good as four – and indeed offer greater versatility for jumps and other dare-devilry – while an ordinary cycle is as good as a motorbike for learning the essentials of balance, control, braking, cornering and so forth. Off-road tracks are more prevalent in the United States than in Europe, for reasons of space and, to some extent,

climate. In the West, nowadays, the chances of taking a
peaceful walk in the countryside are becoming increasingly
remote, especially if you are in the vicinity of a city of any size.
Anywhere within twenty miles of Los Angeles, San Fransisco
or San Diego, for example, you will be attacked on your rural
promenade by a furious bee-like noise emanating from a
swarm of bikers. It is a sound that can carry some distance, and
you may be able to avoid meeting them. On the other hand,
you may suddenly turn a corner and uncover a whole buzzing
nest of crash-helmeted teenyboppers leaping off high
hummocks, swooping down sharp inclines, fording streams
with a panache extraordinary in someone who can't be much
more than six years old.

The off-road cult has spread north to Canada, where the local vehicle for acts of daring – and interrupting other people's country walks – is a skidoo or snowmobile. Some of these vehicles, like some of the bikes, are not all that cheap to buy, and a certain amount of parental complicity is usually needed. This is not often a difficulty, since Dad tends to be a sucker for the new toys and, having paid for them, feels quite entitled to have a thrash on them himself.

It's the same on water. Anywhere in the world, unless you pick your bathing spot with great care, you are under constant threat nowadays of being mown down by some speedboat, jet-ski or ski-bike. They are at it in the air as well, zooming around in hang-gliders and ultra-light aircraft. The thrills that once were enjoyed on the open road may now be experienced in all kinds of other places – and particularly by those who are too young to take a powered vehicle on the road.

I see this as no bad thing at all, because those kids are gaining a lot of useful knowledge which they will be able to apply positively when they eventually take out a licence to drive a car. At the same time they are getting rid of that wild exuberance which is not an ideal quality in a responsible road user.

It is risky. Of course it is. But it is my contention that these are worthwhile risks. Historically, it is the mother's role to fret and worry, and maybe blame the father for buying his son – and sometimes his daughter – a motorbike. Our own family policy is to let our sons have motorbikes – but restrict them to off-road use. We know they can be hurt – and indeed a neighbour, a fine healthy young man of 23, is now paralysed as a result of doing no more than my son might do any weekend. But we accept the risk; we expect there will be a few spills. We also strongly believe that parents ought not to wrap their children in cotton wool or they will end up never doing anything on their own: never going to school or on vacation on their own, never cultivating an appetite to do any of those normal 20th-century things that cannot be learned from books or in the classroom.

When it comes to driving, I recommend parents to let

their children start with cycles and motorbikes, and build up their skills slowly, learning to control power and use it positively, and so gain essential confidence in themselves. If they make mistakes they may have to pay for them, whether by skinning a nose or a knee or even breaking a bone. But if the parents make sure their children have the right equipment –

the right crash helmet, the right gloves, the right boots to support their ankles – then, with a little bit of luck and a good bit of help from Above, the chances are they will come through it all right. What is more, they will come through it having done all their wheelies, having turned their machine over a couple of times, flown up a grass bank – done enough, in fact, to make road driving appear mild, insipid even, compared with what they have already done off-road. That way, they should turn out to be more mature, more responsible highway users.

Positive proof has already come from the USA that off-road skills can pay wider dividends. The Americans have recently produced one of the finest crops of young motorcyclists in the world, and look set to dominate in motocross in years to come. Because of the greater emphasis placed in the USA on recreational life, the five year-old on his monkey bike has loads of time to grow into a balancing genius who at fifteen is an extraordinary rider, and by nineteen may be in contention for the world championship. Alongside him are countless others who do not quite have his potential but who have sharpened their driving skills to a point where they can only be better performers when the time comes to take out a driving licence. This must be a heartening sign for the future – everywhere.

THE
GOOD LEARNING
GUIDE

The
time has come for your children, or your girlfriend,
to take some driving lessons. They have reached the
qualifying age, and the cash is available to buy a first
car provided they pass the Test. Here's what you do:
Stay out of it.
Driving instruction, like any form of tuition, is
a task for professionals. The world may be full of willing
amateurs, prepared to give up many hours of their
spare time to free tuition. But kindness is no substitute
for competence, and the simple fact is that the worst
form of driving instructor is the boyfriend/husband/
lover/next-door neighbour. If they have no training as a
driving instructor, they are not qualified to do the job.
Also, in many instances, their motives are less pure
than the newly fallen snow. What tends to motivate
them most strongly of all is the idea that they may be
able to put an arm round the fledgling motorist, or,
better still, feel her leg while she is reversing.

It reflects a pretty poor state of affairs that people should view the business of learning to drive with such levity; but they do. Moreover, they do so in the full knowledge that death or injury on the highway are more likely to claim them, or their pupils, than any bomb from the skies or deadly disease. In other words, people are prepared to commit the ones they most care for to the open road with little thought for their ultimate safety.

Over the years I have become increasingly convinced that highway education has to begin long before people even start to think of fixing on their L-plates. It is a part of education that cannot be left any longer to chance encounters – the odd visit to the school by the local policeman, or a quick scan of the Highway Code before adding another badge to the cub or brownie uniform. What is needed is something far more systematic: nothing less than the addition of highway education to the school curriculum.

Learning about roads, and the machines and people that use them, should begin in kindergarten and continue right through to school-leaving age. To start with, each child can learn in the context of his or her experience. Comic strips and posters can be used to teach pavement drill; the way moving vehicles behave can be demonstrated with a humble tricycle or pedal car. From there, the child can progress to bicycles, mopeds, motorbikes and, ultimately, to motor cars.

Obviously, many schools already possess and display visual materials concerned with road safety. My point is that they are displayed passively, not brought into the full-time learning process. But if they did feature as part of a series of orthodox lessons dealing with both the theory and practice of driving, pupils would come out at the end of their school careers with an invaluable fund of knowledge that they could not have acquired under any other system. They would have learnt what it is like to control all those vehicles, not just once or twice but regularly throughout the seasons of the year and in all kinds of weather. We teach our children to read and write, to keep themselves clean, to believe in our gods. Why should we not prepare them better to deal with the elements – which are a continual threat to their lives?

Future car owners would begin their driving careers with a real understanding, for instance, of the motorcyclist and his problems. Whether they intend to own a bike themselves doesn't matter; by that stage they would have ridden one in sunshine, rain, and in various difficult conditions, and they would be a great deal more conscious of bike people than the current generations of highway users manage to be.

Other sections of the learning programme would teach an awareness of how various machines worked, and how to maintain them properly so that they would be both functional and safe for all seasons. At present we delude ourselves if we think that the general level of our mechanical knowledge is anything better than appalling.

That this is so is not because such knowledge is difficult to come by. It is because we have so thoroughly neglected it in the past. Taken in easy stages, across the span of a school career, every pupil should be able to absorb the necessary modicum with no great pain or strain – and become a far better citizen.

ANATOMY OF AN ACCIDENT

There is also scope for a whole range of projects, designed to expand the future highway user's awareness of how our road systems work as part of the social framework. If you take, for instance, the 'Anatomy of an Accident', there are all kinds of ways to improve our understanding of what actually happens, and of the effects on people and services.

When an accident occurs, what caused it? In around 90 per cent of accidents, it is human error. In this case, was it human error, if so, what went wrong? Was it the injured person, or a third party, who was responsible? Was it, perhaps, a mechanical failure? A tyre burst? This by itself would make an intriguing and rewarding field for analysis by a group of secondary-school pupils.

From there they can move on to procedures. Let us assume that the accident services – Police, Fire, Ambulance – had to be summoned. When someone dialed 999, what actually happened? How was the call channelled to produce, minutes later, the right people at the right spot? Who were they? How many people came? How long was it before the ambulance arrived, emergency aid was given, the injured transported to hospital? How many police cars attended? What did they do? Did they measure up the scene, who did they interview, what did they do with the information?

Back to the hospital. Who was there to deal with the emergency? How many staff are kept on 24-hour alert? What had to be done?

Then there are the costs to consider. How many man-hours were taken up by the police, fire and ambulance services? Who pays for those costs, and how? Move on to the insurance companies. What actions did they have to take? How much did it cost them?

If a lawsuit took place, what was the outcome and what effect did it have on the parties directly involved? What happened to those people – to the person judged responsible, to the victim who was not at fault but whose health, ability to work, domestic circumstances, were seriously, or otherwise, affected?

What a lot of question marks! And this is not intended to be a full-scale checklist, just a few pointers to the many elements involved. Surely, though, they all have a bearing on highway education, and the issues that young drivers would be well advised to know something about before they themselves pull out into the thick of the traffic.

BACK TO REALITY

Meanwhile, in today's world, beginners must learn and someone must teach them. I have already outlined the first way *not* to do this – by allowing parents, boyfriends, etc, into the act. The next-worst way is to go to the rip-off driving academy.

In the majority of countries today, the standards required before someone can appoint himself a 'fully qualified' driving instructor lie somewhere between the woolly and the non-existent. In Britain there is a register, kept by the Department of Transport, of Approved Driving Instructors. Unfortunately, admission to the register, or acceptance as a trainee instructor, is far too easy. That, at least, is the contention of the 26,000-strong Driving Instructors Association, a private body which lobbies continuously for improved standards of training and a broader-based programme of driver education.

In the absence of more positive leadership from Whitehall, the DIA is currently formulating its own professional diploma, to be obtained in conjunction with colleges of technology and other educational bodies. This, it hopes, will not only enforce a higher level of qualification, it will also bring about a change of attitude among the learning public, making more people want to go on and become advanced motorists, and discouraging the low-level view held by people who say: 'Great! I've passed my Test. Rip up the L-plates. I've finished learning.'

The chief problem at government level seems to be that driver education is a politically unrewarding ticket. At present rates of progress, a minister would have switched jobs or vanished from power long before a real programme could be worked out and implemented. A period of several years would then have to elapse before it could be seen whether the scheme was in fact producing results. And the results themselves – better drivers, fewer accidents, fewer lives lost on the roads – are not the kind which politicians tend to see as 'productive'. In other words, they cost enormous sums to achieve but do not tip anything back into the coffers of the reigning government. Meanwhile, the view of most people now actively crusading for better highway education and better road safety is that governments doggedly persist with an outmoded set of negative priorities. They do not, in my opinion, spend nearly enough on ways of educating the next generation of highway user. This means that the newcomers are unlikely to be any better than we are – and look at the numbers we kill and maim on the roads each year. This is not just a British, American or even a Western problem – it is a global dilemma.

JAPAN SHOWS THE WAY

The Japanese have a success story to tell which emphatically demonstrates the rewards to be gained from highway education. In 1970 they had an abysmal road-safety record; by 1980 the death rate on the roads had been halved.

In that ten-year period the Japanese had sought drastic improvements in two principal ways. They drew up a register of officially licensed motoring schools, and they introduced road-safety instruction in schools. The Japanese character responded eagerly, and there is now a disciplined control about their approach to driving, particularly in their choked and overcrowded cities, which was notably lacking before the government blew the whistle.

Learner-drivers begin their course of instruction at an off-the-road school, where they might spend their first twenty-or-so lessons driving slowly round an artificial road network, with pedestrian crossings, traffic lights, and so on – beautiful to look at but unnaturally peaceful. Then they take an interim test which determines whether they can go on and complete their learning course with ten more lessons, now driving on the open road. Not only must the transition be a shock, the schools themselves are only open during normal business hours and many Japanese cannot get to them; instead they get their instruction on the black market, at one of the many unofficial schools which now handle about 20 per cent of all learner drivers.

Nevertheless, the road-accident figures make it clear that Japan as a nation has had a big change of heart since 1970 about driver education, and about road safety in general. If you consider that there are some nations in Africa where you can take out a driving licence after a few sessions of pushing Dinky toys around a tabletop layout, with no practical driving required at all, then you can see the horrifying gaps that exist between one country and, conceivably, its neighbour. Imagine what happens when the drivers of two such nations come together. A recipe for undiluted chaos.

THE RETIRED MOTORIST

In March 1935, the driving test was introduced in Britain, since when little has changed to keep up with the times. Despite huge changes in car efficiency, quality of roads and traffic density – which by no means cancel each other out – the testing system remains much as it was. Not only that, once a British driver has got a licence it is his or hers until they are seventy, regardless of how their brains or bodies may alter in the meantime.

The Japanese could not be expected to approve. Recently a British delegate at a motoring congress was tackled by two Japanese colleagues.

'How often,' they wanted to know, 'does British car go in for checkup?'

'Once it is three years old,' replied the British delegate smartly, 'every car must be checked once a year at a government testing station.'

'OK,' said the Japanese. 'Now. British driver. How often does he go in for checkup?'

'Oh, well . . . never,' said the British delegate.

The eyes of the two Japanese narrowed even more than usual behind their spectacles, which were both of the thick, bottle-lens variety.

'But what about eyes?' one of them demanded. 'Eyes get worse.'

'I know they do,' said the British delegate. 'But in Britain there is no checkup unless you have a serious illness and have to get a doctor's certificate. Otherwise, you can go on driving without any form of test until you are seventy.'

'Huh!' gasped the Japanese, unable to comprehend a system which allowed driving licences to be held indefinitely, and by right rather than by any proof of merit.

I am very much on the side of those two short-sighted Japanese gentlemen. I feel that a system of re-testing has to be introduced eventually, whereby everyone must go in every so often and, at the very least, have their eyesight checked. At present, though, the testing authorities are overburdened with their current workload, government money is scarce, and it looks as if we shall have to live for a few years more in the company of that contradiction in terms – the retired motorist.

At his best the retired motorist knows his capabilities and does not seek to exceed them. If he is ill, or his eyesight deteriorates, he gets himself checked out in a responsible manner.

At his worst he is belligerent, frustrated and intolerant. He 'knows' how to drive and will not accept advice. He is easily maddened by traffic jams and the congestion that is a fact of daily life in our towns today. He thinks – and here he is at his most dangerous – that his many years at the wheel have earned him a divine right to brake or change direction without warning, and to go at any speed he pleases.

Talk to any taxi-driver working in a retirement area, say one of the English coastal towns. He will tell you first that he is an extremely brave man to be doing what he does, and lucky to be alive after the four to six incidents he next tells you about. At the end of your journey, you may be convinced that the most dangerous figure on the modern highway is not the boy racer, the Hell's Angel or the Belgian coach driver: he is the nice little old man next door, who, by the way, has never had a driving lesson in his life.

KINGS OF THE ROAD

E**very**
driver has his place. Most drivers tacitly accept this,
even if they cannot always agree where they themselves
belong in the great motoring hierarchy.

If we begin with the assumption that a good
pro is better than a good amateur, and that a good big
pro is better than a good smaller pro, it is safe to assert
that the truck driver is *the* king of the road. He is a
supreme professional; he may drive around 150,000
miles a year, and the machines he operates for his living
are certainly the biggest on the road. In his travels he
accumulates a vast store of highway knowledge. He
knows where everything is; he knows all the best
transport cafés across whichever continent he is
required to drive, and where the best-value beds and

other comforts are to be had. From his elevated perch
on the road he can smell danger a good two miles away,
whether it be in the form of an idiot – some whizz-kid,
say, or a tourist or holidaymaker meandering about
from lane to lane with a swaying caravan in tow – or an
accident or some other hazard. In sunshine and snow,

hail and lightning, he is out there trucking all through
the year and he *knows* what's going on.

    The truck driver risks being thought arrogant
by some other-rankers, particularly if by some
mischance he has just blown them into a ditch while
overtaking them. These things do happen, but in
mitigation I would say that there is a great deal more to
driving a large articulated truck than there is to
operating a family saloon. The larger they are, the
more impressive the feat. This truth was borne in on
me recently when I met the man who might justifiably
have claimed to be King of Kings. We were at
Goodyear's test track in San Angelo, and he was driving
the world's largest motor vehicle.

This $1.5 million earth-moving mammoth had an impressive maximum speed of 50 mph. Its giant tyres seemed as high as a house and cost an owner $60,000 each time he needed a new one. Apparently he was happy to do this, reckoning that the benefits of being able to shift 200 tons of earth in one vehicle outweighed using several vehicles of lesser might. The fuel bills must have made his eyes water, though; not for nothing did this mega-truck have a colossal 450-gallon fuel tank fixed to its side. With a locomotive engine revving to 11,000 revs, the wheels could not have been expected to turn very far per gallon of juice.

At any rate, I drove this monster, and can only say of its full-time driver that he was an artist – definitely my choice for Monarch of the Quarries, if not for roads everywhere.

FOR HIRE/NOT FOR HIRE

Taxi drivers are by nature cliquish. Arrogant too. There is a basic assumption that people should make way for them because they are who they are. This seems to be a universal characteristic, as does the tendency to concentrate in particular locations – usually towns and cities. To my mind they are all the better for sticking to their own patch – there is nothing quite so out of place as a London cabbie in the midst of rural England.

No city can be easy to know intimately, but I continue to be astonished by the professionalism of the London taxi-driver – he of the square black cab – and would certainly put him at the top of his class.

People say you cannot get a London taxi if any one of the following circumstances applies:

a) It is raining.

b) Your destination is more than six miles from Westminster Bridge.

c) Your destination is in the opposite direction from the way the taxi is pointing when you hail it.

d) It is late.

e) The driver is hungry.

I would reply that this has not been my experience – with the exception of the rainy day. I also feel that some taxi users invite

trouble through a certain lack of consideration. Who, for instance, in his or her right mind would march up to one of those green-painted refuges, tug open the door and, through the cloud of bacon fumes, presume to say to the huddle of men in anoraks and quilted waistcoats clustered anxiously on narrow benches round a table laid for twenty: 'Now, which one of you is going to take me to West Norwood?'

To more sensitive taxi users with tales of misfortune to tell, I would add that only on very rare occasions has a London cab driver had to ask directions to my destination. Their knowledge of the city's streets, avenues, crescents, alleys (you name it) is truly remarkable. What is more, the cabs are kept clean, both inside and out. The ashtrays, for instance, are almost always emptied regularly and often. And the vehicle itself is superbly built for its particular function – something you will not find anywhere else in the world, except for the odd few British cities, such as Glasgow, which also use the London type of cab. So, if you can once master the art of not sliding off the back seat to land bump on the floor in a cloud of parcels when the vehicle stops in a hurry, you should have a happy experience with the London taxi.

The odds are not so heavily in your favour in New York. The famous Yellow Cabs may be uniform in colour, and from a distance as you emerge, say, from one of the airport buildings at JFK, a row of them looks really rather smart. As you get closer, you cannot help noticing the dents, the rust, the sad air of decrepitude that hangs over them. The interiors are uniformly filthy, the upholstery is hacked and splitting, the quality of the ride – as you jerk unpredictably from one lane to another – is both spongy and disquieting, and your host, perhaps the first New Yorker you have ever spoken to on home soil, is probably one of the rudest, most disobliging men you have ever come across. And Iranian/Russian to boot.

Some travellers find New York taxi drivers hilarious. They love them. They pass over the rudeness, preferring to see it as razor-edged metropolitan wit. 'This is how it really is in the Big Apple,' they say to themselves, relishing the murk and grime, and the heavy wire mesh screen separating them from the driver to reduce his chances of being mugged, and the mean cubbyhole through which they feed their fare at the end of the journey.

I prefer the way they do things in, for example, Las Vegas. Maybe it's because the weather is warmer, but you can be sure that as you approach the cab the driver will get out, open the door for you and put you safely in. It must be a better way; it gets the journey off to a good start, and the customer can bask in the happy notion that he or she is as good as in the limo class.

Limos are decidedly one up from taxis. In high-pressure societies and professions such as showbiz you have little hope of being thought someone if you do not have a gleaming limousine waiting to scoop you up at the airport. The limos themselves compete to outdo each other in length, lushness, plushness, acreage of tinted glass, grandeur of television sets and cocktail cabinets, and general bad taste. The drivers carry their own distinctive identification. Those who work for Celebrity Limos in New York wear a bright red tie, for instance, which actually is a very sharp idea because it does away with the need for nameboards and all the other cries and body language which drivers and clients otherwise have to submit to in the cause of making themselves known to each other. If you know you are being met by Celebrity Limos, just look for the guy in the red tie.

There is, by the way, a third method of getting between Manhattan and the airport by hired car. This other species is known, rather confusingly, as an airport limousine. It is neither cab (costing about $23), nor luxury limo ($65), but a kind of stretched multi-seater which you share with maybe ten other people; your luggage is strapped to massive roof racks, and if you are prepared to put up with the loss of privacy the same journey need cost you only about $8. The world's longest car, the 1962 Chevrolet featured in the *Guinness Book of Records,* might have been built with this role in mind – though with its overall length of 32ft 4in it might also have provoked excited reaction in the downtown traffic.

COMMERCIAL FAILURES

So far, the law governing who stands at or near the top of highway society seems to be governed by the machines people drive. The truck driver earns respect in direct proportion to the size of his device, and the classic taxi driver claims his place by virtue of his vehicle's singularity.

Whether in London or New York, taxi passengers are segregated from the driver – either for design reasons, as with the London cab, or to safeguard the driver's skull, as they like to do in New York. This quality of remoteness is important. You don't exactly have to make an appointment to speak to your driver, but you have to lean forward in a rather ingratiating way, and perhaps also you have to tap on the glass or wire to attract his attention; if your message is then deemed unpalatable, it is surprising how easy it is for the driver to go deaf on you. Inevitably, this increases his stature in his own eyes.

Solo drivers of other commercial vehicles do not score nearly so well. The van driver enjoys few privileges on the road. He occupies a kind of no man's land peopled by unfortunates who have failed to mature into truck drivers. Bakers can sometimes rise above the lowly station of van drivers on the compassionate grounds that they are up and about at first light or before. A milkman, on the other hand, could not hope to succeed with a plea based on his unsocial working hours; it is too widely known that most milkmen drive *electric* vehicles – and that is something no serious driver would ever do.

It is even worse for the commercial traveller. No matter how much he may fancy his prowess at the wheel, and no matter how many tens of thousands of miles a year he may drive, he does not even qualify for consideration. As long as he drives a 'plain-clothes' vehicle, i.e. one with no livery or markings, he is thrown in with the pile of *ordinary* motorists, who, of course, come nowhere. 'But look,' he may say, desperate for higher status. 'Look at all those samples I carry in the back. Anyone can see I'm a *real* commercial.' 'Nuts,' comes the implacable reply from above. 'You drive a nothing motor, you're nobody.'

A brief note should be included here about bus drivers. Brief because I am sad to have to report a steady decline in the status of the bus driver. In part this is because he has been overtaken by technology. Not long ago the London double-decker was one of the most impressive sights on the road; nowadays there are dozens of vehicles that are not only larger and heavier but also carry a greater visual impact.

Television has not helped. Too often the establishing shots introducing some Third World capital focus on a rickety old bus, from the sides of which hang at least fifty grinning freeloaders like so many strands of spaghetti.

This kind of spectacle does little to enhance the image

of the serious bus or coach driver precisely at a time when his status should be on the rise. For is he not the man who can transport you, say, from London to Glasgow in six hours at negligible expense, while you lie back in total comfort, reassured by the presence of a functioning lavatory, watching video films and accepting food and drink from delicious hostesses? He is indeed! But the long-haul man is part of but a small minority among bus drivers, and we shall have to wait and see whether that minority can arrest the general slide.

PLUS AND MINUS

The only chance for members of the 'ordinary' group of motorists to step out of their class is to possess a car that by its velocity and power claims special attention. Such attention would probably be accorded, for instance, to the driver of a Porsche. Drivers of Ferraris may also expect their claims to be recognized. The only problem with a Ferrari driver is that he is usually old; the cars are so expensive it takes years to buy one, and if he persists and eventually succeeds he will be accused of being an old codger trying to recapture his youth. He may further damage his claim by being a rather poor driver. He may in fact end up with more negative points than plus points.

We have not mentioned negative points before, but a minus scale does indeed exist. The reason it exists is that there is a category of driver whose outstanding characteristic is that he or she is dangerous. (The male chauvinist view would have it that nearly all women feature strongly on the minus scale, but in fact, women are more conscientious drivers; they regard their cars with a certain awe, which is diametrically opposed to the macho approach but which actually makes them *safer*.)

One class of driver who lives deep among the minus points has no female counterpart. He is the boy racer. He is instantly recognizable by the sound and fury of his gear changes and his open exhaust pipes. Drivers with any kind of plus rating have his number immediately. He is the person for whom the phrase 'steer clear of' was invented; it is impossible to predict what the boy racer is going to do next – turning right, for instance, or left, or both; accompanied in every direction by burning rubber.

YOU RANG, SIR?

The chauffeur is a strange bird. Real chauffeurs should not be confused with limo drivers, however luxurious the limo. The distinguishing mark of the real chauffeur is that he is in private or executive service. He works for one person or family and no-one else; the idea of being attached to a common pool of drivers makes him sweat at night.

Alone among the more highly rated drivers we have met, the chauffeur wears a uniform. Current taste is for a grey suit and cap, white shirt, black tie and shoes. The uniform both makes him stand out and is a main source of his social problems.

Chauffeurs are notorious for their social problems. When they stop for refreshment, few watering holes are suitable. No chauffeur can go to a transport café; he thinks they are beneath him anyway, and he *knows* he will be derided for

his uniform. In a motorway restaurant complex, he sits alone at a corner table in the medium-price grill. He would not dream of mixing with the rabble of ordinary motorists in the self-service section. On the other hand, even if he can afford it, he cannot go comfortably into a quality restaurant because someone of the employer class is bound to notice him and say disdainfully: 'But isn't that so-and-so's chauffeur? What's he doing in here?'

Chauffeurs have a high rating as drivers partly because they are such mysterious, silent figures. They are by no means all good drivers, but the best can purr round corners confident that their master's newspaper will not even twitch; place a glass of water on the dashboard, and not a drop will be spilt.

It is probably the air of effortless Jeevesian superiority which they exude while driving that makes other motorists give them privileged treatment, such as letting them cut across their bows at Hyde Park Corner. There is an opposite view, however, which regards chauffeurs as appalling snobs, traitors to their humble origins, etc, etc, who have far too many privileges already and should be carved up whenever an opportunity presents itself.

The best chauffeurs love their charges and clean and polish them daily. Better than anyone they understand the secrets of polishing, and do it without leaving a fingermark anywhere. They know, instinctively, not to wipe a windscreen which has misted up on the inside because once the demister has done its work the marks will remain until the whole windscreen has been chammied down again. Who else knows such things? (I heard it from a chauffeur.)

The very best chauffeurs, the aristocrats of their calling, do not wear grey suits at all. However, they are curiously reluctant to let the lower halves of their bodies be seen in public. This is because they are chauffeurs to the Royal Family. They are given blue suits to wear, and are seldom seen outside their vehicles for the magnificent reason that it is not part of their job to get out and open doors. Oh no, sir. Another person does that.

POSERS AND PASSION WAGONS

Motorized courtship has always been competitive. After his first solo ventures the male novice soon realizes that mere possession of a driving licence and the irregular use of his mother's Mini are not in themselves enough. As he sits alone in a corner of the café, ignored and quivering with lust, he knows he must do better, must get himself a Passion Wagon.

In the choice he makes, and how he decorates it, he needs to resolve several dilemmas. First of all, he has to show a fine awareness of the nature of the market in which he proposes to deal. This is much more important than the décor, which comes later.

The main choice is between speed and commodiousness. By observing which girls go with which machines, he will soon be able to tell whether in his locality speed is a critical factor. If it is, he needs a sports car. If, on the other hand, the more laid-back comforts of wall-to-ceiling carpets, divan, bar-fridge and post-coital television set are indicated, then only a van will do.

It may be some while before he can afford to lay hands on either of these. In the meantime his best move is to get an old banger and dress it up, installing more sumptuous seats from other cars, applying new paintwork, go-faster stripes – anything, in fact, that will increase the vehicle's singularity, its essential voojiness. With luck, the day will soon come when he is able to invest in a main-choice vehicle.

SPEED AND THE COFFEE-BAR COWBOY

I had a Volkswagen van somewhere in between the Austin A30, the A35 and various Austin Healys that I drove in my first licensed years, and I can vouch for the VW's efficiency as a mobile bed-and-breakfast establishment for a single young man on the razz.

But in the crowd I circulated with – the coffee-bar cowboys of Dunbartonshire – it seemed that speed was a better commodity than comfort, particularly if you were trying to pull the more up-market kind of passenger. After some energetic months of preliminary research and development in the back seat of the A35, I was lucky enough to be able to move on to an Austin Healy Sprite. Lucky because none of these cars I drove actually belonged to me: they were usually demonstrators from the garage or borrowed from my father.

The Sprite was the cheapest and smallest form of device with which you could elevate yourself to the sports-car bracket; it bore out the truth of the saying 'You get what you pay for'. In order to get close to a young lady from head to toe, you had first to sit with her in the bucket-type passenger seat, put the car into third gear with the handbrake off, push the driver's seat forward as far as it would go, then manoeuvre gently backwards until your head and shoulders, and hers, were in the boot. Provided she was neither too tall, nor too wide, this was a quite workable arrangement.

The only real problems arose if you were disturbed while in the reclined position. Given that this was likely to happen at any time in a 24-hour period, it was a sensible precaution to have a printed sign fixed to the upper part of the boot's interior which warned every young lady not to raise her head suddenly to try and look out. Unwanted visitors trying to see into the car were usually frustrated by the steamed-up windows, but if, in response to a call ('Jean! Jean! Where are you?'), the young lady arose sharply upwards, the inevitable *ker-doink* of skull on boot would betray our dispositions to all the world.

LOOKING THE PART

Speed gave any would-be poser a start over the other motor merchants in our coffee-bar crowd, but looks and style also counted for a great deal. If you aspired to being any kind of poser, you needed an open-top car *and* a car radio (then a wondrous novelty) which naturally you played all the time at full volume. A friend of mine, Allan Jones, had a PhD in posing: he drove an ivory Mercedes-Benz 190SL; it had a radio in it, and Allan decorated himself with an Austrian felt hat which had badges pinned all over it. (As an additive, by the way, we all believed that the fertility of the *car* was increased if it too carried a full-frontal display of badges, preferably in jeweller's enamel.)

My own chief claim to sartorial suavity was to be one of the first people in Dumbarton, ever, to wear trousers without turnups. This was a spin-off from going to compete in clay-pigeon shooting events on the Continent, where most trousers were sold without turnups (it was also decidedly one-up at that time to buy your clothes abroad).

One day I saw a man at a golf club wearing suede brogue shoes, which struck me as the cat's pyjamas in footwear; it cost me several weeks' tip money from the petrol pumps to buy a similar pair in Glasgow. I was never into scarves. The long wispy silk thing flying out behind in the wind seemed

altogether too poncy. Cravats, worn with a dark-blue double-breasted blazer, were fairly pompous-looking too, but I quite liked them and bought several, wearing them tucked inside a powder-blue zip-up windcheater which, I felt, greatly enhanced my desirability. How times have changed!

In this slightly random way my youthful motoring wardrobe was assembled. If it conformed to an overall image it was possibly a relaxed version of the *concours d'élégance* style which may still be glimpsed today – at owners' club rallies, for instance, and down Surrey lanes on Sunday mornings, where the motorist and his vehicle regularly park on the forecourts of chi-chi tudorized pubs while he in his blazer and flat cap drinks pints of bitter from a mug with a handle which he never uses, preferring to grip his 'jar' in horseshoe style from the other side. In this, as in his dress, he demonstrates his unquenchable enthusiasm for a purist mode of behaviour.

Regrettably, his breed is on the way out, destined for ultimate extinction because the sports car itself is all but a thing of the past. Names like Lagonda, Riley, Alvis, and, most recently, MG, have all but faded from view. It is unlikely that they will rise again, except as expensive fibreglass replicas, which are not the same thing at all – as any nice girl will tell you.

BUT WHAT WILL MUMMY THINK?

The old-fashioned sports car driver stopped the hearts of many a middle-class mother. Not necessarily because she fancied him for herself (though she would not have been unmindful of his 'fighter-pilot' qualities of dash and adventure); of greater concern was what he might do in terms of bodily damage to her daughter. So, while socially he might have an A-B rating, he was also a greater or lesser actuarial risk according to his Prang rating. This was ascertained separately by a few well-directed telephone calls around the neighbourhood. If the Prang rating was not too horrendous, then the best strategy of the prospective mother-in-law (all mothers are prospective mothers-in-law) was to hope, cajole or bribe him into concluding that the forthcoming financial strains of matrimony must prise him loose from sports cars and force him to investigate the hitherto despised domain of the safe saloon (a predicament discussed more fully in 'The Family Way', below).

The gradual demise of this amiable demon of the road has brought the middle-class mother increasingly into contact with a greater range of motorized suitors. By another form of measurement, an updated version of the Prang rating which we will call the Terror Arousal scale, she has learned to

distinguish between many categories of merchant, from the Safe to the Unsafe to the Over My Dead Body, and several others in between.

Most reassuring of today's batch of motorized suitors is the quiet young man who arrives in a modest, well-preserved machine, say an old model Escort. Initially he is almost sure to be greeted with favour. 'Isn't it sweet? Isn't it clean? Who did you say his parents were?' Provided he is not a wolf in sheep's clothing, with a carpeted van parked just round the corner, to which he ferries desirable spinsters of the parish in the Escort, rather as a tender plies between the dockside and the sin-cruiser anchored in the bay; provided, too, that he is not as deafeningly boring as the mouselike smallness of his motor might indicate, then this young man should go far. In fact, he is in danger of going too far too soon, and finding himself standing at the altar in a penguin suit years ahead of schedule.

Less easy to deal with is the apparently well-meaning but highly scruffy individual whose battered and neglected vehicle may or may not reflect the true nature of the owner. Is he aristocratically careless, or does he really like having one door a different colour, or shade of rust, from the others? Will all the cars he ever owns smell of pipe tobacco and mouldering dog? Happy the prospective mother-in-law who finds that this young man behaves the way he does because his parents are so wealthy that he doesn't need to care what people think.

What if, on the other hand, the vehicle drawing up outside the young lady's house at a quarter to twelve on Sunday morning is a little more . . . suggestive? Suppose it is a red Mustang, with big looming pipes and number discs on each side, a wing on the back, an airdam at the front surmounted by masked headlamps and a barrage of spotlights? If she is at all a responsible and loving mother, the sight of such a vehicle will immediately register three danger stars on her Terror Arousal scale. Any voyage her daughter has contemplated making with that young razzaway is to be avoided. Even if she does not lose her baby altogether, realizes the suddenly panic-stricken mother, she is bound to be assaulted or taken advantage of in some dastardly way before she is released again at the front gate. Owners of this kind of Passion Wagon soon discover that there is more to owning a rapid-transit vehicle than just driving it. They must acquire many other talents, not least of which are diplomacy and toad-like powers of flattery, if they are to get even as far as shepherding the girl out of the house and into the car. If they do not possess and ruthlessly apply these talents, they will fail. They may even end up staying to lunch! A mother with three-star Terror Arousal will stop at nothing.

An even chillier welcome awaits the all-out *rich* speed merchant. As soon as he undrapes himself from his expensive motor-car – a Porsche, perhaps, or a Ferrari Berlinetta with the roof open – the mother is not just worried. She is horrified. She just *knows* that the horrid boy is going to be smooth; that he is sure to silver-tongue her blameless daughter into a downward spiral of unspeakable acts; that he must already have done some awful things to less moral daughters; that he is undoubtedly on some awful drug, marijuana at the very least, or cocaine, if he can afford a vehicle of such opulence. Whatever dreadful balloon dreams may have sprouted from her head on sighting the owner of the red Mustang, that young man did have the doubtful merit of being an undisguised lecherous rascal – a creature she can identify and deal with. But this one! With this one it can only finish in tears at the Law Courts. On her Terror Arousal scale the Porsche-Ferrari poser rings up four red stars, a rosette, and three pairs of knives and forks.

So who gets the girl? At this point we have to say that all generalizations are invidious, but . . . If we had to pick one winner, he would be a fairly calculating middle-of-the-roader, driving something like a last-model Cortina. The car should be clean but not too clean. It should not, for instance, bear signs of tyre paint; wheel blacking is the mark of a fusspot (a more obvious sign is if the boy perpetually dives under the bonnet before any journey can begin). The car will have the best seats (curiously, prospective mothers-in-law react positively to smart upholstery; they seem to view a back seat rather as they would view a sofa in a furniture shop, without reflecting on the uses to which its owner will strive to put it). The car will also have good sound equipment, and will be used to play some music at peak volume which is not hard rock. Scarlatti, for instance, is OK at any volume.

What about the boy himself? What will he *look* like? Well, here the mother can usually relax. This is the daughter's territory. Provided she and the boy are operating in the same market, they will follow one of the dozen or so current and ever-changing styles of dress and will look compatible when they are together. Details of appearance are less ritualized and rigid than they were in the heyday of the *concours d'élégance* sportsman described earlier. People may dress down for effect, or they may dress up. The state of their wallets can be a decisive factor.

There is little more to say about the physical appearance of the motorist himself, except for one thing. It is my contention that a girl is more turned on by someone who looks clean and smart than by someone who is deliberately crumpled or blasé. Girls almost universally dislike lack of cleanliness, and if the boy overdoes the tacky, oil-stained look he risks being thought unclean also. Unless, of course, the girl herself is by inclination tacky and oil-stained. In that case they are operating in a different market altogether – and deserve each other.

UNDERCOVER OPERATIONS

If *the* image of sexually attractive speed is an open-top sports car, the epitome of the laid-back and commodious Passion Wagon is a van. A van, moreover, with superb sound equipment, carpeting on walls, floor and ceiling, swivel armchairs, a water bed, dark dark windows and a huge airbrushed exterior decorative scheme. But before we reach that near-ultimate womb-on-wheels, there is another evolutionary stage we must look at. The pickup.

In the United states the pickup is *the* young man's vehicle. In its small two-litre versions it is both cheap and economic to run (around 36 mpg) as well as socially acceptable. Although in Britain the image of the pickup is working-class – that, say, of the plumber's apprentice – and a fundamentally unthrilling sight for our middle-class mother when it draws up outside the house on a Sunday morning, American mothers see the thing through different eyes.

Provided, as ever, that the vehicle and its driver are clean, American mothers of blameless daughters tend to say to themselves: 'Now look at that boy in his neat pickup. Fine way for a boy to start. You can see his father didn't spoil him with a heap of money to squander, but I guess that family must be doing pretty well all the same. So that's fine if he wants to take my daughter out.'

The philosophy is entirely different. But then Americans are less hog-tied by traditional demarcation lines of class, and entirely unfettered by the Great British vintage-car syndrome. Instead they have the custom bug.

The custom business has now reached massive proportions, and organizations such as SEMA (Special Equipment Marketing Association) hold their own shows in places like Las Vegas where they exhibit a sea of bolt-on goodies and psychedelic strips. There, in between the obligatory brass-band fanfares and the friendly hustling of a horde of bikinied beauties, you can see pickup trucks that look like Rolls Royces inside, or are built to resemble nothing less than a Panzer division tank. Those, roughly, are the two extremes – of charismatic flash and all-out machoism – within which the custom market flourishes in all its garish splendour.

This commercially agreeable state of affairs has come about because manufacturers and promoters, even in sedate Detroit, recognize that there is a virtually bottomless youth market out there, just waiting to be tapped. And the first thing you hit them with is a pickup.

American flatbed pickups have a bizarre glamour. As leisure vehicles they are half useless in that no-one does anything much in the back. The passengers all crowd up front in the cab, listening to the bellowing of the CB radio and hollering their own call-sign: 'Tartan One here, breaking on Channel Two-One, looking for a northbound 18-wheeler. How does it look over your right shoulder?' (This is Jackie Stewart. Will that truck I just passed report on any police up ahead.)

Pickups come in many sizes, and a large number are built way off the ground so that they can go across almost any terrain and never have their axles touch Mother Earth; they have oversize wheels and oversize springs, and you really need a step-ladder to get up into the cab. External gear, in addition to the waving plantation of CB antennae, includes a formidable battery of lights which, from any distance, resembles a horizontal Christmas tree as it bears down on you. Some of the lights, operated from a central control panel that can only have been designed at, or stolen from, NASA, are positioned on the roof of the vehicle; they are essentially searchlights, some of them are coloured, and their chief apparent function is to observe the movements of the planets through the night sky. Beneath the front bumper is another range of lights. These are very slick to look at, but owing to a communications malfunction in the design team (meaning that no-one said anything to the electrics people about this vehicle going off-road) their life-span is generally short; the first time the pickup runs into a bush or sand dune, the entire sub-bumper unit is wiped off. This is particularly regrettable in that it also damages the aesthetic balance of the whole frontal appearance.

External decoration is essential, but necessarily limited in scope by the size of the vehicle. It is really in the next category of young man's wagon – the van – that external decoration comes into its own.

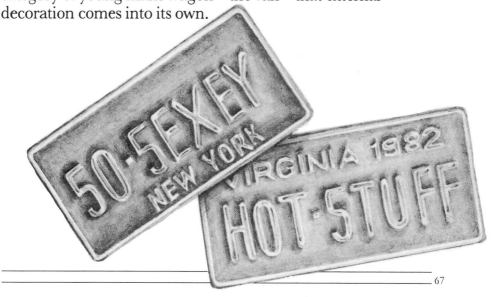

The form it takes will usually reflect the owner's interests. If he is a hunter (as they say in America), the sides of the van may carry a great artistic rendering of a hunting scene with antelope, moose, wild turkey, quail, etc. If he is into rock music, the side walls will be ablaze with logos, brand names, album sleeves redepicted in giant airbrushed versions, and all manner of supportive psychedelia.

By virtue of its greater size the van is also much more suitable as a venue for round-the-clock passion. For whereas the small pickup's cab offers little more room to manoeuvre than a sports car, and can only come in for serious use after dark at, say, a drive-in movie, a van can be as secure and secluded as a hotel suite no matter what the hour.

Behind its heavily tinted porthole windows the well-appointed van is a carpeted haven, with additional décor in leather or velvet or some other unambiguously tactile material. Speakers for the stereo system generally hang from the roof. The altar of passion is, ideally, a water bed. Large vans may also contain a video tape deck, and swivel armchairs for both rear and front seat passengers so that all can rotate themselves into position for a communal discussion when the venue is reached, or while they are parked and resting somewhere.

As will be evident from this, the van has the further advantage that it can transport the gang. Some form of gang transport is highly desirable. It has always been one of life's great pleasures, especially among the late teens/early twenties age group, to travel with a group of friends, piling into the back of a bus or van and taking off for a rowdy tour of the local fun spots. There is also considerable kudos to be had from owning the vehicle which selflessly tracks between the drive-ins and all-night cafés, the discos and the parties – and can also be relied on for the occasional trip to the mountains, or down to the beach. It is inevitable that all new and shapely members of the gang will eventually take a ride in the van. If they can then be induced to travel up front . . . who knows what agreeable surprises may be in store?

A SAD BUT TOUCHING FOOTNOTE

There is one further category of vehicle that by its size and general luxuriousness, its couches, showers, fridges, heaters, air-conditioning, etc, should be the ultimate in Passion Wagons. This is the old-style RV (Recreational Vehicle), and it is represented in the United States by such makes as Winnebago, Superior, AMF or GMC. Indeed, had the young people of the Western world become seriously involved with RVs before now, the populations of those countries would be far larger than they are. Unfortunately (or perhaps the reverse) Nature in her wisdom has made RVs generally too expensive for the pockets of the young, and these excellent, plush and remarkable wagons are instead identified with middle age, with families, with Golden Oldies on camping trips. On summer nights, as he gazes into the embers of the camp fire, there is nothing a Golden Oldie likes more than to recollect in tranquillity what feats he used to get away with in his various vans and pickups – back in the Good Ol' Days.

THE
OTHER
FELLER

I_t is never entirely one's own fault, is it? Some smidgen of blame must always be ritually smeared on the other driver, no matter what the circumstances. It is pride more than logic which seems to demand it; self-respect, and a primitive desire to cover one's tracks, outweigh the desire to seek a more intelligent solution.

In this chapter I want to look at some classic driving errors which all too often lead to accidents. By the time we are through, it should have emerged that the inclination to error begins long before the accident. It begins in the garage at home, before the car has moved an inch.

Compare an airline pilot, doing a detailed and exhaustive set of pre-flight checks, with a bleary-eyed businessman stepping straight into his car

on a Monday morning. Half a piece of toast still hangs from his mouth, and he may give one of the tyres a kick as he walks past, a brief gesture intended presumably to wake up the machine. He is Mr Sloppy, and he has no eyes for the taped-up broken tail-light, or the near-bald offside rear tyre. He is quite proud of the ingenious way he has stuffed a coathanger in the aerial, and it is normal for him to enter via the passenger door because the door-post on the driver's side is dented out of true and the door will not open.

He climbs inside and starts up. He is oblivious to the sordid and dangerous scene which surrounds him in the driving compartment. This is awash with rolling drink cans, baby rattles and fluffy toys, and the rubber mat beneath his feet has rolled up beneath the pedals so that the brake cannot be depressed for more than two-thirds of its intended travel. So much for *his* pre-journey checkup.

The airline pilot may be what is termed a professional, but the businessman's 'amateur' status does not give him licence to claim he is anything less than 100 per cent responsible for his car when he is driving it. However, with awful regularity it emerges that the 'amateur' car-owner has only the most basic grasp of the machine he is driving. So how can he be 100 per cent responsible for it?

Take winter driving. During the last spell of heavy snow, I found myself watching an unfortunate neighbour who could not get his car up the incline to his garage. Moments later he went into the house, fetched some pieces of carpet and wedged them firmly behind the back wheels, got in and started the engine.

The result was not at all what he had been counting on. Wheels span all right, but still he had no grip; no forward movement. The only flaw in my neighbour's plan was that he had been working on the wrong wheels. Quite unbeknown to him, he had somehow bought himself a front-wheel-drive car – and had never managed to catch up with the fact.

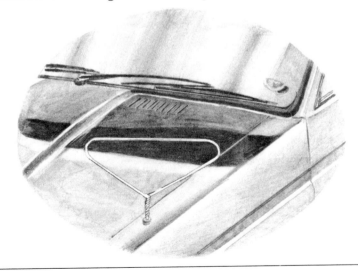

THROUGH THE SEASONS

There are so many things that drivers can do, before they set out from home, that will make their lives infinitely easier, and safer. Winter is the time when more extremes occur, and more can go wrong – through damp, through freezing, through suddenly-arriving, impenetrable drifts of snow.

Heavy snowdrifts are mercifully rare in Britain, but that does not mean we should not have some knowledge of how to cope with them. Someone observed recently that the British not only had a good accident record per user mile, it was *twice* as good as some European countries that might have been expected to do considerably better. He cited Austria, which combines modern roads with a disciplined and well-informed driving public. What he had omitted to consider was that the Austrians have to contend with icy, treacherous conditions for half the year, and with mountainous hairpin routes all the year round. If British drivers had to cope with that lot, their accident rate could be expected to soar well beyond the Austrians', and remain there at least while they got used to the 'new' climate and terrain. And while it is true that the British do not get a lot of practice at driving in snow, they know it is going to happen occasionally and that life will be difficult when it does happen, so why not wise up to the problem in advance and save a lot of trouble later?

Drivers should aim for optimum visibility at all times, but in winter the problems are more acutely felt. The good news is that today's cars are vastly better equipped to deal with snow, fog and heavy winter weather than ever they used to be. Electrically heated rear windows, now that we have them, can be seen as a truly invaluable aid; like windscreen washers when they first came in, they once seemed something of a luxury, but now we cannot live without them.

Few cars now capable of passing the MOT test are not fitted with a ventilation system adequate to clear the car thoroughly. People forget, unfortunately, to make the best of what they have. If they allowed just a few minutes in the morning to blow air round the car, they would have far fewer problems when they were actually out on the road.

Another thing: do your washers squirt straight in winter? Or are they the kind that get partly glued up and then pee all over the car behind? Not very efficient, is it? It doesn't wash a lot of windscreens, for sure. It's also a trifle disturbing for the following driver, sat there at the traffic lights while this gusher comes sailing back over your roof and starts beating on his bonnet like two tomcats piddling on a corrugated iron shed.

If this should happen in summer, there are – invariably – added embarrassments. The liquid in the washer bottle has turned brown since it was last changed. It is not actually raining; you have simply pressed the wrong button. The car behind is driven by an attractive girl wearing a sparkling new, mainly white, summer outfit; she is on her way to a garden party, or possibly to Ascot. She is driving an open-top sports car and your sepia-toned spray sploshes straight in her lap. Even though you did not mean to discharge this effluent all over her, it *looks* like a real tomcat's revenge. She certainly thinks so, and a policeman is just now crossing the road towards you.

Not all seasons are as demanding as winter, but relief – usually premature – at the arrival of spring can lead people to do daft things, such as forgetting to take off their winter tyres. Spring is usually both wet and slippery, and the adhesion available from winter tyres is not nearly so good – unless they are special all-weather tyres. This would become rapidly evident in an emergency.

Spring is a useful time to check tyre depths. Some of the worst wet-weather accidents happen as a result of aquaplaning: once your car has taken off on that sheet of water, you are no longer in contact with Mother Earth and there is nothing you can do to save yourself. Whether or not you aquaplane in the first place depends very much on the depth of your tyre tread, and how good your tyres are, and these are things you can control. All tyres are made with certain road conditions in mind, and some tyres are more prone to aquaplaning than others. What may be fine for the arid depths of Arizona will be of little use to the British driver. He should be looking for tyres that are designed to cope with wet, slippery weather conditions, since he can expect some rain on the roads at most times of the year.

The safest way to look at tread depth is not the traditional one of: 'I see it's got some tread on; should be good for another couple of years.' A more sound basis is to regard the minimum legal depth as not worth having. The fact is – and you don't have to go breaking your neck proving it – that the adhesion you get from marginally legal tyres is nowhere near what you need for driving in wet or slippery weather. Such a tyre may look good enough, but if you measure the tread and get barely the 1 mm depth required by law – throw it away. Remember that the tyre you are looking at relies on its tread to move water out of the way to make the surface dry enough to give a grip. At 60 mph on a wet road, the tread pattern needs to shift one gallon of water per second; double that in heavy rain. Look at *your* tyres and ask yourself if they can do that.

Another way to stay out of trouble in wet weather is to avoid driving too close to the kerb or roadside. That is where most of the water lies and, therefore, is potentially the most troublesome part of the road. In towns, especially, you also risk splashing the world as you churn up all the puddles, and this is a category of carelessness that the leading car nations are now recognizing as an offence. (Just because no-one in your area has yet been done for it, doesn't mean you won't be the first.)

When the hot weather comes, new problems station themselves round the corner, ready to ambush the unwary. In summer the heat melts the tar on the road; so along comes the local authority with a gravel truck. A fresh load of chippings is offloaded on the sticky surface, to hold it down and give drivers some extra bite for their tyres. In the night it rains and all the chippings are washed to the side – or else they find their way naturally to the side over the next couple of days. The first person who then goes off-line and arrives on that fresh bed of scattered chippings will think he has turned on to an ice rink and will weave and slither all over the place.

Autumn is *the* slippery season. Not only the leaves from the trees but also the sap finds its way on to the road and can make life highly precarious. Autumn roads possess that additional quality of seeming to have two surfaces: a thin dry top layer masking a damp and dewy undersurface; it's a highly dangerous combination, particularly because you can't see it until you're on it.

NIGHT LIFE

Here are many hardy perennials, which it can do no harm to re-examine. Let's begin with the windscreen wipers. If they are not working properly, say because the rubber is perished or bunged up with grease, driving efficiency at night can be whittled away drastically. In fact, it would be better not to use the car at all until the wipers have been put right.

At night the driver must see as well as be seen. If it is raining and his vision is continually impaired by oncoming lamps planting highlights on his windscreen, it is no joke. If the outside mirrors are dirty and unusable, that is no joke either. Nor is it if the headlamps are cross-eyed and focused to beam somewhere up at the trees – all right, as they say, for low-flying aircraft; less than good for cars.

There is a curious myth that if a driver puts his headlamps up, he will see more. Wrong: because all he will get is the reflection of his own lamps back in the windscreen. We met some extraordinary lamps in our earlier survey of 'Passion Wagons': those mounted in many-coloured clusters on the roofs of pick-ups, for instance, admirably demonstrate their uselessness in bad-weather conditions every time they are switched on. The other battery, mounted low – the ones that get swept away in bushes and small trees when the vehicle goes off-road – are much more effective for seeing the road ahead either in darkness or fog because their beams travel forward at the appropriate angle.

Lately a lot of people have become altogether too attached to fog lamps. Possibly they were attracted to them in the first place by their dubious qualities of macho brilliance – 'Wear these and everyone will look at you'. Whatever people's motives, they should remember that fog lamps are too powerful to combat anything except thick fog. Used against mere rainfall, they are a menace, creating dazzle and havoc wherever they go.

. . . AND A FEW SURPRISES

No survey, however brief, of ways in which drivers can keep themselves out of trouble would be even halfway adequate without some warning about the sheer unpredictability of other drivers.

Some categories of accident – when turning right, for instance – are well charted and imprinted on the minds of most drivers who, as a result, should have half an eye on the possibility of danger each time it seems likely to arise. On the other hand, what can you do about those inexplicable acts at the wheel which come under the broad heading of 'Eccentric Feats'?

Specifically, there is probably little to be done. In general, though, it is a good idea to keep your idiot-detector equipment switched on at all times. Drivers who manifest one eccentric habit usually have several others in their repertoire, and it is as well to be on your guard if you find yourself behind one.

From my youth spent in and around the garage in Dumbarton, I can recall at least three eccentrics of the old school. Each had his own special form of aberration, but the

real difficulty for other road users was knowing in advance
when he was going to do it.

Old Mr Gow was a sweet man, but when he moved
off from stop it was something to hear. We knew about him at
the garage because, at the petrol pumps, he would take the
engine of his Rover up to about 10,000 revs, hold it there, then
slowly slip the clutch out and shriek away in a haze of scorched
clutch plate. We also knew about him at the garage because he
kept destroying clutches. He referred, incidentally, to his gear
stick as the 'clutch lever'.

'My motor car is not going well,' he would complain,
'the clutch lever's gone again.'

This was simply because, when he put it into first
gear, the car would not move. On just one Rover he went
through seventeen 'clutch levers'. Clearly, he was not a man to
walk in front of when he was about to get under way. His type
still lives. Beware.

Another of the Dumbarton crowd had a block about
cyclists. He could never remember to look behind when he
parked to see if anything or anyone was coming. As a result, he
batted at least four cyclists into the middle of the road with one
swing of his door. Others he would cause to nosedive by
innocently whipping open the door just as they came up
behind. His type still lives (it's known as 'bike-bashing').
Beware.

The third type is probably now extinct, so rare was his particular quirk. Other people throw things out of car windows, but this man was rather special. He threw electric cigarette lighters, and what is more he never did it intentionally. The problem was, as he plucked a new one from the dashboard of his 3.8-litre Jaguar and lit his cigarette, he kept forgetting that these lighters were not quite the same thing as matches. Down would go the window, out would go another expensive electric cigarette lighter – followed moments later by shrieks of agony and wild curses as he realized that he had jettisoned his only source of fire for the rest of the journey. As Jaguar dealers, we got through more electric cigarette lighters because of that one man than anyone else in the distribution network.

Few people hurl such exotic junk from their car windows nowadays. All the same, you never know. You may never know until it hits you.

THE FAMILY WAY

Few individuals can be more pitiable to behold than Yesterday's Flier. His courtship days are over; wedding bells have clanged; a family has arrived; the rent/mortgage and household bills require a vast outlay of money that he used to spend entirely on the good things in life, e.g. bolt-on extras for his Passion Wagon.

As the buff envelopes arrive daily to pollute his doormat, he finally has to admit that there are not enough funds to provide for the extravagances in life as well as the ordinary, boring things he must now be responsible for. Not only must he satisfy his wife's requirement to be housed decently after she has gone to the trouble of leaving the comfort and convenience of her parents' place to set up home with him, there are the two lots of parents to consider. In the interest of future dividends, they must be reassured that he is serious about his new station in life. Sadly he reviews his balance sheet.

A sacrilegious act is called for and one momentous day he commits it. He sells the chrome razzle-dazzler. The replacement is a used dark blue Marina with a vinyl roof. Next payday, as a gesture to his glorious past, he buys and fits a plastic louvre to the rear window; at least it does not now look exactly like every other used Marina in town.

He, unfortunately, is himself beginning to look a little bit used. He still wears his shiny jacket dedicated to a now-slightly-over-the-hill rock band; his hair is still long and he has not relinquished his patched and faded drainpipe jeans. His options, though, have narrowed considerably: where once he drove on Sundays to a succession of pubs, clubs, parties and barbecues, his destination now is either the in-laws' house or the zoo. As a rocker he has, decidedly, gone off; so, poor girl, has his wife, since she has by now endured the pains and physical ravages of childbirth. Any keen observer, watching them troop past the Monkey House with the pushchair, would be forced to conclude that at least one of these impoverished souls had not wanted to be really married in the first place.

It is the low period for both of them. Their circumstances will improve with time, but what they once had is gone and they will never get it back.

The upturn in their fortunes is signalled to the rest of the world by the departure of the Marina and the arrival of a brand-new Fiesta. Promotion and a timely switch to another company bring yet better things, most notably in the shape of an XR4 Sierra.

Our British ex-Flier naturally has an American counterpart. He has suffered similar agonies followed by gradual improvement; in his case the gleaming Corvette was jettisoned for a used Mazda, which was replaced by a larger used machine – a Fairmont. Reaching up again, he gets his hands on a Mercury Topaz.

On either side of the Atlantic, two essential moves remain to be made. The first is to put the wife on the road. This is done either by turning one of the early rejects over to her or, preferably, by buying her an estate car/station wagon, which in the first instance might be a five-year-old Escort/Pinto and which is invaluable for the school run and for trips to the out-of-town discount store.

The second and much more significant move – because of its enormous potential for boosting the ego – is to add a third car to the stable. This will be a performance machine, and will enable him to recapture the image of his youth. In the United States this process of re-establishment can be satisfactorily achieved with a Mustang, a vehicle which by itself represents a chapter in the history of American masculinity. In the UK, well, who knows . . . a used Porsche would do quite nicely, would it not?

COUNTRY TYPES

The estate/station wagon is the ideal vehicle for the more ambitious type of family outing or holiday. Their build makes them especially popular among country dwellers who are less concerned about the constrictions of urban parking spaces. But you do not need to live in the country, of course, to play the country squire.

Many country squire look-alikes work in the City, or are lawyers or newspaper executives; they live in the outer suburbs and the estate car they mostly favour is the Volvo.

At a typical Volvo event, say a point-to-point meeting, the Volvos line up side by side as far as the eye can see. The contents of vast lunch hampers are spread out in the space formerly occupied by the two golden retrievers, and the family set about eating and drinking themselves into a mild stupor before going to place their bets on the first race. Teenage offspring sit on the roof and wave their Lady Northampton boots in the air whenever they sight a chum. It is all a little inbred, this Volvo-eventing; its scope extends also to other equestrian events, including polo, and to the more significant rugby matches, where the picnic is taken in the car park before the game. (Soccer matches are also attended by Volvo estates, but their owners are electricians or plumbers who use their machines chiefly as weekday work-horses; they do not go in for picnics.)

Other acceptable large estate cars are made by Peugeot and Ford (the Granadas). The latter, though, are

usually confined to up-market users, particularly in the plush
Ghia version. Buyers include the Royal Mews, so adding
further to the Ghia's 'top-drawer' image.

In the United States the station wagon reached the
final stage of its evolution some while ago in an awe-inspiring
series of dinosaurs characterized by huge overhangs and the
handling ability of a pregnant elephant. Covered in wood –
plastic wood – and with a seating capacity of up to eleven, they
have roof racks as big as ornamental gates. When it is vacation
time, the roofs of these mammoth wagons of yesteryear –
Chryslers, Chevrolets and LTDs – are carefully loaded with a
sufficient declaration of affluence, sometimes packed in a
special plastic bubble; the weight of it also ensures that the
nose of the beast pokes sharply up in the air. At night, with the
lights on, this is known as the Owl-watching Effect.

A myth that has long accompanied these wallowing
monsters states that they offer better-than-average protection in
the event of an accident because their structures are more
easily deformable. This may be so, but it overlooks the more
significant fact that it is precisely because they flop and wallow
to such an extreme degree that these wagons become involved
in accidents which almost certainly they would have avoided if
they had been a bit more agile. In any event they are a dying
breed.

Their successors are altogether smaller, and sportier.
They include the Chevrolet Blazer, the four-wheel-drive US
equivalent of the Range Rover, and the Ford Bronco. Ford also
produce a Bronco 2, which is smaller still and a very useful tool
for towing a horse box, for example, or for a skiing expedition,
or for going off to hunt duck, wild turkey or quail, or for
cruising to rural events such as the big country fairs of Middle
America. Jeep, International Harvester and a small swarm of
Japanese manufacturers are just some of the companies now
getting into this market.

Bigger than these are the Recreational Vehicles or
RVs – the Winnebagos, etc – which are designed for camping
and touring in total luxury. They are the ultimate in comfort,
with couches, fridges, air-conditioning, canopies, TVs, videos,

superb stereo: all, in fact, that a Golden Oldie could wish for –
and it is for him and his expanded wallet that these vehicles are
principally designed.

Many a Golden Oldie has a family with teenage
children who aspire to their own Passion Wagons. Either that,
or he is still just about hanging in there as a middle-aged
hippie, socially acceptable by virtue of his weirdness rather
than his sexual prowess. Both types in fact accept that RVs are
not suitable for pulling women – though they are wonderfully
comfortable for sitting in and thinking about it (the old spark
has gone). Meanwhile the task in hand is usually to entertain
and cater for others, ferrying the young to off-road motorcycle
meetings, for instance, and maybe carrying some bikes in a
trailer hitched behind.

One of the great sights of American outdoor life is the
scene at the big desert races, the Baja, for instance, or the Las
Vegas to Reno. You come upon an entire city of Recreational
Vehicles, with Dad, Mom, Uncles, Aunts and countless
children all camped in Occidental splendour somewhere near
the cookout. They are there to watch Junior perform in the
race, but while they are at it they make sure they have
themselves a fine old time.

An indispensable part of such proceedings is some
kind of drinking vessel. Everyone, young or old, at all times
must carry a drink. People not going around with a drink in
their hand are certain to attract a social stigma which will be as
difficult to shake off as the Old Man From The Sea. The habit
is akin to smoking a cigarette in order to keep at least one hand
occupied. Not everyone smokes, however, and so carrying a
drink, usually in a plastic cup, is the generally safe answer to
this social dilemma, providing an essential halo of confidence.

The contents of the drinking vessel are almost, but not
quite, immaterial. If it is 90 per cent filled with ice cubes, that is
OK. There is no law which says there *must* be alcohol in there,
and in fact it is quite acceptable, in the early part of the day at
least, to lope about with a coffee. Thereafter, it may just be
better to opt for alcohol. People can be funny. Beer is very
useful on these occasions, and is *the* male drink for some sixty

per cent of waking hours. Soft drinks are acceptable for women throughout the daytime, preferably with a twist of lime for added social status; though with the approach of cocktail hour it is prudent to exchange the soft drink for something stronger. Soft drinks for men is a more complex area. Probably they are best avoided. Diet Pepsi, in an off-road desert setting, is a highly non-virile substance that you would be seen with at your peril. At the other end of the virility scale is the man whose beer is never quite the same colour as other men's beer; the unspoken thought is that he likes to refresh himself with a slug of something extra. This invariable qualifies him for that most dubious of ranks, 'a man's man'.

HOME CAR CARE

If the sales of motoring magazines are a reliable indicator – and as a group they are second only to women's magazines – then few families can be without at least one car-care enthusiast. There are, however, varying degrees of involvement.

At the bottom of the ladder is the man for whom buying and reading the magazine is enough. He may be just idle, or the kind of intellectual dreamer who by the time he has finished reading an article about changing an oil filter, actually believes he has done the job himself. He thinks that cars are quite pleasant objects, and wishes his own was in better condition. He is a Theory Man.

The middle range is occupied by a fairly large wedge of the population who like to spend Sunday morning cleaning and polishing their car as a preamble to a round of golf or a trip down to the pub. The hallmark of this merchant is that he is non-technical. Under the bonnet, he just about knows which one is the battery and several years ago, after lengthy manual reading and much frustrated cursing, he found and filled the bottle for the windscreen washers. He lives in dread of puncturing while on the road, and changes his car as often as he can possibly afford because that is the easiest way he knows to have nearly-new tyres under him at all times. In his reading of the motoring magazines he is concerned with cosmetic/economic matters. He is a Car Consumer.

At the top of the ladder are two very different types. It

would be invidious to say which was the better man, but both earn their high rating because of all the owners we have so far encountered they are the only ones who actually attempt to carry out mechanical works.

First is The Modifier, the front of whose house is instantly recognizable because it looks like a scrapyard. Depending on the size of his garage/workshop, and what the estate agent years ago referred to as his 'front garden', he keeps upwards of three cars at a time, rebuilding them gradually from parts he has garnered from professional scrap merchants. It is a gradual process, because he never seems able to concentrate long enough on any one project. There are parts to be bought or scrounged, back numbers of *Exchange & Mart* to be gone through (he has a pile of them on the garage floor), and long, highly technical conversations to be had with fellow enthusiasts and any neighbour who will listen. This all takes hours out of the weekend and explains, for instance, why for the last three years the red Mini has been awaiting major surgery out there on the bricks in all weathers – next to the cement mixer (for an extension to the garage that he one day plans to build), the radiator grill off a Lanchester which he quite liked the look of, the exhaust system off something else, and two rotted sides of a timber rabbit hutch.

He wants to get down to some serious dismemberment of the Mini before it rusts to pieces of its own accord. But the thing is, he first has to find room for it in the workshop. At present he is building a sort-of Cortina from the remains of an earlier model twice cannibalized for previous work, and some pieces of a Zephyr which he had kept back after another transplant job. Next in line after that, he has an MG in the back garden, but that cannot be touched because thrushes have penetrated its flapping roof and are nesting in it.

All in all, work on the Cortina project has been going very well, really – twenty-one months so far – but just last Wednesday his nephew crashed his motorbike and now he's got that to do. What is more, his nephew is the pushy type and has been hanging about the garage asking when it will be ready. As any Modifier knows, that is simply not the point.

The Modifier, like his cars, seldom leaves his garage.
Nor does he see much of his wife, but this is more through
absentmindedness than deliberate policy. In the matter of wife
evasion he is an innocent compared with the other car-care
enthusiast. He is Mr Egotrip: a fastidious customer. Some
parts of his workshop look like Dr Kildare's operating theatre.
Ranks of spanners line the walls, each one outlined in white to
show up any vacant spot instantly. Neat shelf units contain
every kind of car-care material, for tyre blacking, for the
chromium, the windows, the vinyl roof, the paintwork, the
woodwork, the leatherwork. He has an array of scents for
spraying the car's interior, and indeed the whole garage works
on the lines of a boudoir for automobiles. The floor is carpeted,
there is always heating when it is needed, and stereo, and a
drinks fridge.

Highlight of the week is car-wash day. For this he fills
two pails with temperature-controlled water. One is for the
preliminary washing-off of the grit that has collected on the
bodywork, the other is for the proper business of washing and
shampooing. Each phase is performed with a separate sponge.
Another mark of his washing prowess is that he cleans not just

the exterior bodywork but inside the doors as well. He has a third sponge for the really mucky areas – under the wheel arches, for instance. He never fails to take out all the carpets, including the one in the boot; he then lays them on his work bench and Hoovers them.

It is a moot point whether this man actually knows much about the workings of his car. If he is reasonably well off, he will have it looked after by a local specialist garage anyway. However, he does like to play with his spanners in between the odd gin-and-mixed, which he sips from a tumbler while reclining in a deep old leather armchair which he loves and went to great lengths to remove from the office waiting room. 'My God, yes,' he thinks to himself, taking another sip, 'if I wasn't sitting here I'd be stuck indoors with the wife!'

FLYING
SQUADS

Police
vehicles have come a long way since Sam Marchbanks
patrolled the Dumbarton area. He drove a steed
rather than a machine – a massive police bicycle
made of indestructible materials, impossible to deflect
from its route even under a hail of gunfire. Such
fusillades were fortunately rare, if not altogether
unknown, in PC Marchbanks's territory – at least, as I
knew it in the 1950s. It must have been reassuring,
though, to know that one's bicycle would not flinch
under fire.

PC Marchbanks was a tall burly man with a
red moustache, and it was his role to ride up and down

the streets and country lanes, which were almost empty of traffic compared with nowadays, and make sure that all was right with the world. The chances of him catching the boy Stewart on one of his illicit driving runs over by Milton Dam were remote, since normally he would only have gone up to this corner of his domain to look for poachers, and this by all accounts was not a substantial part of his routine; no doubt the steepness of the climb also contributed to keeping him away.

Now, thirty years on, contrast the spectacle of PC Marchbanks with the patrol cars of Europe and North America, ablaze with lights, bristling with radar guns and automatic cameras, the patrolmen themselves loaded down with dozens of items of gear, and you might think you were on a different planet. It is not so much that the police forces of the world have been especially clever in keeping ahead of the game. Naturally it is their job to try and do so; but what many people find hard to realize – even if they themselves have lived through it – is the sheer extent of the motoring explosion in that period.

THE PICKET FENCE
My own more earnest confrontations with The Law were

fortunately few in my early licensed years, even in foreign lands. Partly I owe this to a sport other than motoring to which I had become attached: clay pigeon shooting.

I took up shooting competitively at the age of fourteen, and gradually began to win selection for the big national and international events. At first, obviously, I was too young to provide my own transport, so it fell to various enthusiasts to ferry me about in their own dream machines. I clocked thousands of miles in the back seats of these usually highly overdecorated objects. To pay them brief tribute, I especially recall the Vauxhall Velox, and the Austin Cambridge, of the Cameron brothers, the former a masterpiece of customized overstatement with super de-luxe fog lights, chromium strips down the body, reflectors everywhere, hand lights outside – a vehicle so immaculately maintained that you could have eaten your breakfast off any part of its interior or, given reasonable weather, its exterior too. There was Andy Thompson and his Ford Zephyr with a Raymond Mays conversion – an astonishing device more like a drag racer than a saloon. There was Bret Huthart, and Allan Jones from North Wales, whose family had an agricultural machinery business that enabled Allan to take out some fairly progressive cars: Jaguars, for example, and an ivory 190SL Mercedes, in those days just about top of the motoring league.

All that travelling may have qualified me as an expert long-distance passenger, but it did little to diminish the enormity of my first big solo drive. The car was an Austin A30, and the task was to take it from Dumbarton down to Bournemouth to shoot in the West of England championships. That was a big deal indeed in those pre-motorway, windscreen-washerless days – about as big, really, as a voyage down the River Amazon. I loaded up with spare cans of petrol, extra provisions, spare parts by the boxful. The expedition was a success. Not only did I get there and back, I also achieved three other cardinal aims: I did not have an accident, I did not need to have a single conversation with the police – and I won the event!

Later I drove abroad to shooting competitions – and

in an earlier chapter, 'The Universal Motorist', I described how I kitted out an A35 with a special front-facing mirror to help me deal with the wily foreigner. All continued to go well, in that I continued to avoid accidents and kept a clean sheet with the police, until the 'Bern Incident'.

I had taken a car over on the ferry from Newcastle to Oslo with Allan Jones to compete in the world clay pigeon championships (and was pleased to finish sixth equal). After Oslo, Allan and I drove down to Bern where the European championships were due to begin a few days later. In Bern they had a Grand Prix circuit laid out on the open road, and when Allan and I got down there we were curious to have a go on it.

My car (a demonstrator borrowed from the garage) was a 3.4-litre Jaguar, metallic dark blue with red upholstery, chrome wire wheels . . . a fairly potent machine but not so remarkable when set beside the 300SL gull-winged Mercedes of Maurice Tabat. Maurice, one of the great shots of the day, was in Bern to represent the Lebanon, and he too wanted to take a turn round the Grand Prix circuit.

From the way Maurice leapt into his car in the hotel car park, it was clear to me that we were taking part in an unofficial race. Once at the course, I had just got myself into the lead when we came to a long left-hand bend. The road surface had been freshly gravelled, and in my eagerness to keep ahead of Maurice I kept the power on and went into a great long, crunching drift. The front wheels stayed on the road, but unfortunately one rear wheel found its way up on the grass verge. The car slid at a good pace, sideways-on to the road, for some distance, and eventually came to a neat little white-painted house with a front garden enclosed by a picket fence. In the garden a grey-haired lady was relaxing in a canvas chair. By now a considerable amount of my car was raised up on the verge – sufficient at least for the back bodywork and the bumper to demolish the picket fence when we reached it. Ping-ping-ping-ping . . . the little white staves were snipped off and flung in the air as though they were part of some high-speed juggling act. Before the horrified gaze of the lady owner, the pieces of her once-immaculate fence cartwheeled in the air, and were returned to earth in the form of firewood.

The decision over what I should do next – stop and say good afternoon or continue on my way – was taken out of my hands as soon as I came out of the drift. For there, on the end of the bend, was a Volkswagen of the Swiss police whose crew had been watching the whole performance. I had to stop.

Behind me, good old Maurice had also enjoyed an excellent view of the spectacle. He too could have been going rather faster than was allowed, but the difference between us was that he had retained control of his car, and just had time and the wit to bring down his speed, nip past the police Volkswagen and bolt to safety.

The police were very efficient. They took my passport away, and were all in favour of taking me into custody for numberless days, despite my protests that I was in Bern to shoot for the British team whose chances would be reduced if I did not appear. This carried little weight when delivered in English from my own tongue, but the British team manager fared a little better. After some extra leverage had been applied by the British Embassy, a compromise was reached. I could leave the police station, but the Swiss authorities would keep my passport for the time being. There was a fine to pay, reasonably enough, and confirmation had to be obtained from my insurance company that they would restore the picket fence in every detail, also compensate the lady owner for a quantity of plants which, it turned out, had been either flattened, sliced in half or whisked out of the ground by the spinning back wheels and thrown in the air along with the fencing materials.

SMILE, IT SAID

Since the Bern Incident, and having no previous convictions, I have been permitted to establish a home in Switzerland. This, inevitably, has deepened my awareness of the Swiss police. They are a curious crowd, supercilious and, for the most part, silent. Visitors do well to remember, though, that the famous Swiss neutrality stops at the frontier. Within its borders the Government maintains a highly sophisticated army and an ever-watchful police force. Like their European neighbours, the Swiss police are armed, and anyone thinking that the gendarmes of a nation of bankers and cuckoo-clockmakers would never use their guns, could be in for a shock.

On the other hand – and this is more in keeping with the cuckoo-clockmaking tradition – they are heavily into all the latest electronic devices for keeping the peace. One of the more devilish innovations is a grey metal box at the roadside which conceals an automatic camera. As you drive past at a forbidden speed, the camera clicks. Two weeks later you receive a photograph of yourself through the mail. 'How nice of someone to take my picture,' is your first reaction; then you notice an accompanying picture showing the needle of the radar gun registering your speed. Gotcha!

STOP THAT HOUSE!

In various other European countries the police operate radar traps, but the position is probably still more confusing for the driver in the United States, where he may have to cross several state-lines. Each state, while keeping to some national norms such as the 55 mph speed limit, also has its own idiosyncratic set of traffic regulations. This applies, for instance, in the various ways they may set and use radar traps.

In what was thought a rather extreme application, a few years ago a householder in Miami was surprised to learn that his house had been booked for doing 32 mph in a 30 mph restricted area. He resented the accusation sufficiently to complain and it was later found that – instead of leaving the radar gun to operate itself, as the Swiss would have done – the Florida authorities had been relying on humans to perform the function. Something was therefore bound to go wrong and, sure enough, along came a car in Miami one day, going a shade faster than it should have been going. The patrolman in charge of the radar gun took careful aim, fired, missed the car and clocked the house.

Houselovers everywhere raised a great scandal, and the embarrassed police retired to lick their faulty trigger fingers. The latest indications are that they are coming round to the Swiss view and putting greater faith in electronic devices of high sophistication. An example of this is a radar gun capable of trapping cars coming *towards* it.

A certain well-known racing driver discovered how this works when he was heading at some speed through South Carolina. He did not notice the radar gun mounted outside the police patrol car which passed him going the other way. But by that time it was too late anyway. The gun had already computed its own forward speed *and* the speed of the approaching car. Next thing our racing driver knew, the patrolman had swung round in the road, switched on siren and lights, tracked him down and stopped him.

There followed one of those strange verbal jousting matches that occur when the person interrogated is prepared to reveal some of the truth, but preferably as little as possible. The well-known driver had a horror of his name being splashed over the newspapers. A speeding charge would do little either for his public image or for his career in the lucrative endorsements trade.

So when the patrolman asked for his name, he supplied his full given names, hoping that the unfamiliar ones would mask the two by which he was known to the public.

The cop seemed not to register. So far so good. 'Occupation?' he asked.

'Retired.'

The cop looked surprised. 'At what age did you retire?'

'Thirty-four.'

'What was your occupation before you retired?'

'I was a driver.'

The cop was now thoroughly suspicious. His jaw muscles twitched to emphasize his mounting annoyance. 'Listen,' he said. 'That's impossible. No way does a driver earn enough so he gets to retire at thirty-four.'

Through the window came the gentle answer: 'I was a very good driver.'

The mildness of his reply soothed the patrolman and the driver drove away with a mere caution. However, it is debatable whether the evidence of the radar gun would have been conclusive. In some states, thanks to the inventiveness of so many American lawyers in getting their clients acquitted, this kind of radar proof might not be enough to secure a conviction. The struggle of the lawyers to hold back the video age has now reached a finely balanced point, but the likelihood is that electronic devices will become more subtle and foolproof while human frailty, including the urge to drive at illicit speeds, will remain around its present level.

SHERIFF OF INDIANA

Although it is still true that one of the most sensible pieces of advice parents can give their children is 'Never accept a lift from a stranger,' I have an alternative version which is for the benefit of adults rather than children. It is quite easy to remember, and goes like this: 'Never accept a lift from a policeman.'

This is not intended as a slur on either the morality or the driving capabilities of policemen. As a group they are good, conscientious, professional drivers – and that puts them at least several points up on ordinary motorists, i.e. the people we usually accept lifts from. The problem with police drivers is that they are distractable.

Don't get me wrong. Many of them are very nice people: they work long, difficult hours and are no doubt highly agreeable to their wives when they have the opportunity. Nevertheless, they all seem to find it immensely difficult to stick to the job in hand. I will give you an example.

I was due at a speaking engagement in Indiana, and for some reason I had accepted a policeman's offer to drive me to the venue. The patrol car was roomy, oversprung and a trifle shabby, but all was going basically to plan when my driver, who was called Joe Harris, nodded his head backwards at a car we had just overtaken, and said:

'That car.'

'Yes?' I said.

'There's something wrong with it. It's kinda suspicious-looking.'

I tried to look back at it without seeming to stare. Outwardly there seemed nothing wrong with the car, but Joe radioed through to get a check on the licence-plate number. The answer, when it came back, was negative: they had nothing on it.

Joe was not satisfied. He *knew* there was something wrong, even if the car was not on the official record of stolen vehicles.

'Jee-sus,' he said between his teeth as he racked his memory for enlightenment, but without being able to say what bothered him about the car, which was still not far behind and which he scanned fiercely every two seconds or so in his rear-view mirror. In the end he decided to back his own judgment against the verdict of the police records. He switched on the siren and lights to get the following car to pull in, so he could take a closer look. The other car, in what was almost a reflex response, took off and swooped past us.

We gave chase. Siren wailing, lights flashing – the full works, as seen on TV plus a wee bit more. In the excitement of the moment, my speaking engagement was forgotten, which is just as well since even a polite reminder to Joe that he really ought to drop me off at the hall before embarking on this new venture, may not have had the desired effect.

We hared down the highway in pursuit of the self-confessed villains. When they shot off down a slip-road, we went after them. We drove into a suburb and I reflected, as a Scot, how apt it was that this should be happening in a town called Edinburg. The chase continued down the main street, up side turnings and into other side turnings, until we came round a corner and found them spinning to a stop, sideways-on across the middle of the road.

It was Monday in Edinburg, Indiana. In the gardens of the suburban street, washing flapped on lines in a faint May breeze. No other people, fortunately, were in sight as my policeman jumped from his seat, pulled his gun from his holster and fired over the heads of the villains who were retreating fast towards a space between two houses. A bullet ricocheted off the roof of one of the houses.

'Stop!' shouted Joe, but his quarry ignored the advice and flew out of sight. He stopped and turned to me (I had made the tactical error of leaving the car).

'Right,' he ordered. 'You go down that side of the

house and I'll head round the other.'

Dumbly I did as he said. Sure enough, I turned round the back end of the house and found myself virtually nose to nose with much the larger of the two fugitives. For some reason I had come round the corner with one finger stuck aggressively out. As soon as he saw this, the man had raised his hands up above his head. Now, as he saw I was unarmed, the hands were beginning to come down.

'Uh-uh!' I wagged my head at him as a warning not to try anything. That froze him for a couple more seconds, then the bluff began to wear off and his eyes were flickering sideways while he assessed his chances. At that moment, mercifully, Joe came round the corner, pushing the partner in crime ahead of him.

The policeman, of course, was making a proper job of it. He had the man – a little guy, about my size (why didn't I get him?) – in a half-nelson and was snarling at him and shoving him. As an extra precaution he also had the muzzle of his gun rammed into the man's ribs.

We got the pair of them into some kind of marching order, and took them back to the patrol car. Both men were then handcuffed to Joe and I sat in front and drove the car back to town.

At last here was something I was qualified to do. The only snag was, I had to work the radio as well, for which I was singularly unqualified. Not only that, but the call sign of the car was... 007!

We drove towards the centre of Edinburg, Indiana, with me at the wheel fiddling with the microphone and calling: 'Hello, 007 to base. 007 to base. We're coming in with two... *(Pause – what do you call them? 'Car felons'?)*... yes, we're coming in with two car felons...*(Crackle crackle from the other end.)* Well, two auto thieves, then...'

Joe, from the back: 'You have to push the button up first if you want them to hear you.'

Me: 'Oh, right.' *(Push up button.)* 'Hello. 007 to base...'

This went on until everyone in the neighbourhood

police force must have been entirely convinced of my mechanical ineptitude. At last we got to the local headquarters, where I was to find that the spirit of Robbie Burns had not deserted us yet. For there, in the yard behind the main building – I could not possibly tell you this if it were not true – the police chief was practising his bagpipes.

The explanation is fairly simple. There is a big Scottish population in Edinburg, Indiana. Perhaps that is why I was there in the first place; not that it matters. The big story is that they made me an Honorary Sheriff of Indiana for my services. To this day I still have my baton, my badge and other trappings of high Midwestern office – and value them greatly.

POLICEMEN NEED SUPPORT

Would I, as a result of that heady success in Edinburg, like to take up policing in the United States on a professional basis? I have given the matter some thought and the answer is a regretful no.

It is really a matter of weight. I have observed American policemen over a number of years and my view is that they should all be issued with shooting sticks. Surely, the load that they are asked to carry is too much for one man. First, there is the walkie-talkie hanging out of a clip; then there is the gun, a large one, slung low in a holster. Then, strung from the belt, which is also worn low, are the handcuffs plus the obligatory bunch of about thirty heavy-looking keys which perform Lord knows what purpose, also the flashlight, and all manner of minor metal pieces. I do not know how any US policeman of average build can be expected to support such a bazaar of equipment round his waist for more than about two hours a day without sagging permanently at the knees. For directing traffic, I feel shooting sticks should be essential issue. On the beat, too, I am sure good uses could be found for them. At all events, I am withholding my application form until this essential aid becomes an integral part of the patrolman's equipment!

HIGHWAY ROBBERY

People who sell cars have the unfortunate knack of pigeonholing a customer the moment he or she steps inside the showroom. If the customer does not come up to the socio-economic mark set by the salesman for his range of vehicles, or if he seems unlikely to want to buy something there and then, he can expect short shrift on the lines of 'Having a look round, sir? I'll be over here if you want anything.'

With that the salesman retires to his desk and noisily shuffles a wad of papers. If a colleague is watching, he will turn to him and toss his head in a brief gesture of disgust. The colleague will nod mysteriously and return to scrutinizing the racing page.

The salesman of course thinks he is an indispensable link in the chain which joins car owners to cars. He never stops to ask how effective he is at selling these machines. New models pass in and out of the showroom with pleasing regularity, and neither he nor his boss – who rose from the ranks on the showroom floor – has ever considered the possibility that they do not actually sell anything. If they were made to consider this unpalatable notion they might find that in the vast majority of cases their marketing expertise has a value of nil; that the decision to buy is made in the customer's mind several days, even weeks, before he sets foot inside the showroom, and that the salesman is in fact an obstructive force as he tinkers irritatingly with the customer's pre-set ideas, trying to sell him extras he does not want, or guide him up the range to another model he has no intention of buying.

The obstructiveness of salespeople was brought home to me the day, not long ago, when I set out to buy a piano for my son. He had reported to me that his piano teacher had been complaining that he did not practise enough. I had asked him why he did not practise. He told me it was because we did not have a piano in the house. I immediately saw he had a point, so we went shopping.

At the one reputable music store in town we were greeted with wide-eyed disbelief and embarrassment when I said I wanted to buy a piano. I realized that I had committed a basic error in piano-customer behaviour. I was not dressed for the part. If you wish to buy a piano you do not go into the shop wearing an anorak and sneakers.

For the next hour I fought my way steadily past a series of obstacles flung in my path by the increasingly desperate salesgirl, who shortly enlisted the support of the manager. After walking about a quarter of a mile we eventually got past all the upright pianos they tried to sell me – each time listing the merits of the piano and the monthly down-payment. As we reached the grand pianos, they went into a crescendo of 'Oh, but you couldn't, you wouldn't . . . not *that* one . . . no, no . . . much too expensive . . . the down payment alone . . .' When at long last I managed to purchase a Steinway for cash, they raised a last-ditch struggle over delivery. 'About two weeks?' they said. 'I want it at the house by four o'clock this afternoon.' 'B-b-b-b-but . . .' they protested, stammering and spluttering. Did this man have no sense of the etiquette of buying a piano?

So it is with cars. The retail arm of the motor industry is riddled with complacency, unjustifiable snobbishness, and plain self-delusion. It is vastly puffed up, over-beveraged, and ripe for revolution. The revolution, moreover, should begin at the top end of the market, for this is the historical stronghold of the reactionary salesman. Let's look at some of them.

THE ROLLS MAN

The executive charged with the honour of topping up the world's supply of Rolls Royces wears a badly fitting three-piece suit. He is of mature years, and indeed his lace-up shoes have been with him for thirty-five of them; he does his best with the battered toe-caps before catching the commuter train which ferries him each morning to the glossy showroom, but the leather is unmistakeably cracking up. He wears a regimental tie, and this talisman of former glory ensures that no-one actually tells him he has dandruff. So he soldiers on. He would prefer to deal only with customers of his own generation – the chauffeurs and regular clients who come to see him every five years or so, and he finds it hard to conceal his disdain for the nouveau-riche businessmen, sportsmen and, worst of all, rock musicians who want to acquire what they like to call a 'Roller', or a 'Roly'.

He is lucky that the British aristocracy have not latched on to the notion of becoming Rolls Royce salesmen. With their persuasive old-world charm, half of them would shoot to the top of the salesmen-of-the-month charts; the other half, of course, would be disastrous – as they are in any case.

THE CLASSIC CAR MAN

He is an old racing driver. He did well to give up the sport before it gave him up, but he has not really found his feet again in civvy street. He wears a British Racing Drivers Club tie, and his own car displays a British Racing Drivers Club decal on the side. He has pronounced tendencies to snobbery but, once the rather chilly overtures are done, he is pleased to tell more or less anyone about the Grand Prix he didn't win.

His *forte* was in fact endurance races, and these for the most part are not widely publicized; he did race at Le Mans a few times, though, and once was the first British driver home, in fifteenth place. He prefers to ignore the fact that Le Mans is mainly for weekend drivers, for the good reason that Grand Prix drivers do not wish to stay out of bed for twenty-four hours at a time and professional drivers are therefore thin on the ground at the hallowed French circuit. He has a photograph in his wallet commemorating his big Le Mans. He won a trophy for it, too.

THE UP-MARKET MODEL MAN

His natural habitat is cloud cuckooland. He is driven to overdo his image by the nature of the product he has to sell. He is dealing in up-market cars and he too must conform with their aura. He must look affluent, act in an urbane manner, and speak with the right kind of accent (public school, classless, and the 'right' kind of regional accent, e.g. Cornish, are all acceptable). He must also project himself in a way that suggests he is entirely at home behind the wheel of the car he is demonstrating – whether it be a BMW, Mercedes, Porsche or something of that ilk – whereas in reality he will never approach being able to afford one for himself.

Somewhere along the line the constraints of this double life – symbolized by the pilchard sandwiches he brings

to work in a red leather attaché case – have produced in him an aloof, condescending manner. Any customer who does not want all the extras on his BMW, or who is prepared to settle for less than the most expensive model, will be greeted with silent incredulity, followed by: 'Well, if that's what you think you want, I'll get the papers.'

He will then walk over to the other salesmen in the showroom and say: 'Jesus. He wants a bottom-of-the-line car, the jerk. I mean, if you can't afford a BMW, why buy one?'

His colleagues all murmur in sympathy and adjust the knots of their Burlington Arcade neckties. It is a cross they all have to bear, sometimes up to three or four times a day. It is, in fact, one of the misfortunes of the up-market motor trade that their product is fatally attractive to so many unworthy owners. This is particularly so in the case of the Porsche.

The typical unworthy Porsche owner (to digress for a moment) works for a large advertising agency. He is good-looking, wears a leather coat with a fur collar and never puts his arms through the sleeves. He wears 24-hour Porsche sunglasses pushed up on the roof of his head, haunts the fast bars and classifies his women as Double A, A, B or C. His car is a disgrace. It is the cheapest model available, and to it he has bolted a host of flash goodies purchased from some 'sporty' accessories shop. No wonder the supercilious gentlemen of the showroom tend to disappear out back when this rhinestone cowboy snakes into view.

THE FORD MAN

Or, that is to say, the BL, Renault, Volkswagen or Fiat man. He exists to sell cars in volume, and is probably the most professional of all those we have so far looked at. To reach the high sales targets he has been set, he has to stay light on his feet and not spend too much time on any one customer. He is democratic, however, and does not mind if you are looking for a Granada or a Fiesta; what he wants is your signature on the order in the quickest time consistent with decency.

His eagerness to tango you across to his desk is a symptom of other short cuts he has become accustomed to taking – in his dress, for example. He possesses a range of ill-fitting light-coloured budget-account suits, and the breast pocket of each jacket is permanent residence for a toning three-pointed imitation handkerchief mounted on cardboard. His shoes are always a shade too fast – coloured grey or blue, or over-decorated with tassels or buttons, or too high in the heel. He wears ultra-short nylon socks which, if they ever got too close to the electric heater beneath his desk, would fuse to his ankles. He does not realize how these and other economies devalue him. Despite his ambitiousness, which may well lead him up the ladder as far as a regional manager's job, or a dealership of his own, he will never lose his flashness. Once a car salesman, always a car salesman.

THE USED-CAR MAN

He is *the* fast merchant – and that has little to do with his cars, none of which has been paid for, all of which he hopes to sell by the end of the afternoon. He lives in a self-induced nightmare of bluff and promises that may or may not have been made and may or may not be kept. He walks on the very edge of the world every day of the week; his brinkmanship far out-teeters anything Mrs Thatcher has yet tried.

He wears a brown hat and a grubby sheepskin coat over an underpressed two-piece suit. At the race meetings he goes to when he is sufficiently flush, or when it seems appropriate to slip into one of life's lay-bys for a few hours, he could easily pass for a bookmaker. In fact, his brother *is* a bookmaker, and they get on very well.

THE AUCTIONEER

It would be a kindness to the general public if a sign were hung on the door of every car auction salesroom, and round the neck of every car auctioneer, saying 'For Pros Only'. This would not stop all the innocents who fancy their chances from having a go, but it would perhaps diminish the number of scenes that go, with a dreadful consistency, like this:

Mr and Mrs Townsend have read in some consumer magazine that if they are prepared to take the risk of buying 'as seen and without warranty' they could well get a bargain at an auction sale. They go down to the auction rooms and are soon excited by the 3.5 Rover that seems to be going very cheaply.

Mrs Townsend, in a whisper during the bidding: 'Oh darling. I think we're in real luck. It's so marvellously cheap.'

Mr Townsend: 'Yes, we'll have to see how it goes, of course. But I really like that colour, and to find the right colour in an auction is just . . .'

Auctioneer: 'Gone!'

For the next hour Mr and Mrs Townsend watch with mounting dismay as a waterfall of cars passes under the hammer, each vaguely possible candidate – the Renault 20, the old but interesting Jaguar, the Princess, the Datsun – being snapped from their grasp by a bunch of lounge lizards who scarcely seem to blink their eyes each time they strike. As Mrs Townsend so aptly puts it during the ride home: 'It's not fair!!'

IN PRAISE OF HEALTHY MOTORING

I_n

Edwardian times people viewed the question of safety on the roads in one of two ways, according to whether they were Dinosaurs or Ostriches.

Dinosaurs were convinced that the new mechanical monsters threatened the entire future of the human race. Laws to protect the British public, as laid down by the Light Locomotives Act of 1896, were seen as woefully inadequate. Already, with the raising of the speed limit to 14 mph, the man with the red flag had been made terminally redundant; where would it all end? How could the exposed human frame be expected to withstand the stresses of travel at such furious speeds? Within a few brief years civilized man would be rattled to extinction.

Rearguard actions were proposed, but they too bore a doomed aspect, well represented by the campaign of the American Farmers Anti-Auto Protection Society which demanded, among other measures, that 'automobiles running on country roads at night must send up a rocket every mile and wait ten

minutes for the road to clear. They may then proceed carefully, blowing their horns and shooting their rockets.' To those bewildered farmers, the automobile was clearly worse than a herd of vile-tempered stallions. Unless their spirit was quickly broken, they would run loose across the land, kicking lumps out of their former masters and eventually – who could tell – Taking Over.

The Ostrich lobby was less hysterical than the Dinosaurs. Its members sought to get round the problem by the traditional method of their species: they ignored it. So, when in 1902 the editors of the Badminton Library added a volume on *Motors and Motor-Driving* to their Sports and Pastimes series, they commissioned a chapter on 'Motor Cars and Health' which had nothing to say about accidents or safety but, with superb blimpishness, instructed its readers on how motoring could actually improve their health.

Its author was Sir Henry Thompson, Bart, FRCS, MB, a veteran of eighty-two who could remember steam coaches running in London as far back as the 1830s. Seven decades later, he welcomed what he blithely called the 'revival of automobilism'.

Sir Henry had little doubt that motoring was good for you. He explained: 'The easy jolting which occurs when a motor-car is driven at a fair speed over the highway conduces to a healthy agitation; it "acts on the liver", to use a popular phrase, which means that it aids the peristaltic movements of the bowels and promotes the performance of their functions.' Writing, in my turn, eight decades after Sir Henry, I can only say that the performance of my bowels has been more effectively assisted by the antics of *other* motorists than anything I can do for myself!

It has taken us a long time, heaven knows, to progress some way from those rival Edwardian stances. Not very far, mind you, and not nearly fast enough; but at last it seems that in the 1980s there is a more general determination to wrestle with the social burdens that we have inherited in a century of rampant automobilism.

THE ART OF BELTING UP

Chief and most pressing of these burdens is, without doubt, safety. We kill more people each year on our roads than we do by any war or by any disease. In 1981, for example, there were 148 million registered drivers in the United States, and 165 million registered vehicles. In that same year 50,800 people died on the roads, and 25,000 of them were in a car when the fatal accident occured. Of the other main groups of fatalities, 9,000 were pedestrians or cyclists, 5,000 were motorcyclists, and 7,000 were in trucks. Altogether, in 1981 two million disabling injuries were suffered on US roads, and the cost in money to the highway authorities, excluding police and court costs, has been calculated at $40.6 billion.

You do not need to be a saint or a statistician to agree that all these are unacceptably high figures. What, then, can be done about them?

One other statistic that catches the eye shows that the

United States has a remarkably low percentage of drivers who regularly wear seat belts. The meagre 11 per cent of Americans who take advantage of the single most useful device for preventing death and injury on the roads, *and the 89 per cent who do not,* make a sorry picture when set beside the figures for some other developed nations.

In Scandinavian countries, where belting-up is compulsory, more than 90 per cent obey the law, as do nearly 90 per cent of Australians. By contrast, the British had a low wearer rate of 26 per cent before legislation came into effect; since, then, while there are no annual statistics available at the time of writing, it seems that fear of a £50 fine has spurred many habitual non-wearers to toe the line.

I have long been a convinced seat-belt wearer, and will not travel any distance – however short – without strapping myself in. What continues to amaze me, however, is the number of people who have no clue at all about how to put on a seat belt.

They watch me slip mine on, and decide out of politeness to follow suit. What follows is pantomime. They wind the strap every whichway but where it should go: they dip their head under it, slip the belt behind their shoulders, round the back of the neck, twist it between their thighs, grab for the buckle and snap it shut at an angle which snarls up the whole apparatus. 'There!' they gasp, looking for all the world like the Great Houdini just after the last chains and padlocks have been secured. It is then my task to untruss them and show them how to put the belt on from Stage One – without, of course, seeming to patronize. It also helps if I can do it without laughing, for these people are in a very delicate mental state as they observe the habits of a lifetime undergoing radical surgery.

What some resent most strongly is the taming of their ancient appetite for self-destruction. To sustain this appetite, they will even go to a doctor in search of a certificate of exemption from wearing a seat belt.

'I don't need that bloody thing,' they harrumph. 'I've been drivin' fifty years without an acccident. Nobody's goin' to tell me what to do . . .'

As we all know, the reason they have not had an accident is that the rest of the driving community have so skilfully kept out of their way for all those years. It is curious, too, that when these same people board an aircraft, they are among the world's most docile creatures, belting up like little angels when the stewardess tells them. At all events, there are rarely medical grounds for the exemption they seek; their battle with the powers-that-be is really one of philosophy.

Women can be just as persistently wayward as men. They listen to all the statistics about seat belts saving lives, then say: 'But do *I* really need to wear one?'

'No,' I have learned to reply. 'No, you don't need to wear a seat belt – provided you can afford £20,000 and don't mind eleven months of plastic surgery. You may never get your face back as it was, but after you have been through a windscreen it will take the surgeon that long to try and fix it for you.'

Recalcitrant men usually bring up the argument that

if there was a fire after the accident, or the car went into deep water, they could be trapped in their seat belts and fried or drowned, whereas, with no belt to hamper them, they would escape. This argument has in fact gained far more ground than it deserves – I suspect because it carries a strange emotional appeal ('With one bound he was free') which has given it a wide circulation. To refute it, we need only refer again to the 1981 US statistics, which show that fire and water accidents, including those started by electrical faults, account for only 0.05 per cent of accidents involving cars. In effect, therefore, supporters of the 'death trap' argument prefer to ignore what happens in the vast majority of accidents, and stake their life instead on a 200–1 chance.

If further evidence is needed in support of seat belts, try this. The impact of the human frame striking a solid object at 30 mph is equivalent to falling from the third storey of a building onto a concrete pavement. So, the next time someone baulks at wearing a seat belt, perhaps on the grounds that they are only going 'round the corner, it's not worth it', you can say:

'OK. If you think you can do press-ups after dropping three storeys, then you can put your hands out and save yourself in a 30 mph accident. But I happen to know you can't do that.'

You might add that more than 90 per cent of accidents occur within a radius of 20 minutes' driving time from home.

SAVING THE CHILDREN

The impact factor is especially acute with children. If they are not properly restrained in the back seat – either in a carrycot which is strapped in, or in a bucket-type seat with its own safety harness, or by booster cushions – then the implications are horrific. In an accident, the unrestrained child is likely to be shot like a bullet against the dashboard, the gear lever or the back of the front seat. Only if it is fortunate will it be flung against the seat and escape more serious injury. In the case of a baby, 25 per cent of its weight is in the head. In the instant of a crash its body becomes a projectile and starts to fly forward, and with so much weight concentrated at the leading edge, the chances of the baby incurring a head injury are frighteningly high. Such injuries are not always immediately apparent; it may take five years for the effects of an injury to become clear, by which time it is rare indeed for remedial actions to be of much use.

Parents are also inclined to ignore that the unrestrained child is a constant menace because of the things it may get up to while it is allowed to roam unsupervised around the back of the car. Picture the child who suddenly thinks it would like to get up and hug the driver, maybe wrapping its arms round his or her neck, or covering his or her eyes, and you will see what I am getting at.

In fact, I am in favour of seat restraints for all, for adults as well as children, in both the back as well as the front seats. Manufacturers are creeping towards this, and now in the United States they must fit seat belts in the back of every new car that is built. So far, there is no legislation that compels people to wear the belts; few do.

CRASH HELMETS

In the UK it is now compulsory for motorcyclists not only to possess a crash helmet, but to wear it. In the USA the law varies from state to state, and some bizarre legal judgments have been recorded. In one case in California a young rider suffered a head injury in an accident, but his insurance company refused to compensate him on the grounds that he had been irresponsible and not worn a crash helmet. The young man took his insurers to court and there revealed that he *had* worn a crash helmet. 'I had it strapped to my leg,' he told the judge, who decided in his favour.

Macho it may have been to go to such lengths to satisfy the law, *and* avoid the indignity of wearing headgear that in his circle must have been distinctly unmodish, but to my mind the young rider had his priorities well screwed up. Despite being a successful litigant, he very nearly became a paraplegic, or a corpse. Someone, I hope, will have revealed to him by now another statistic of the road: nearly a quarter (23 per cent) of all motor-bike fatalities happen to people not wearing crash helmets. On their heads.

FROM RUST-PROOFING TO IDIOT-PROOFING

Despite its proven appetite for self-destruction, the human race has survived its first century of automobilism remarkably well. We will continue to produce a sub-species of lemming whose members ritually drive themselves at full speed into lamp-posts and over cliffs; but the rest of us have suffered little in the way of fundamental damage. Contrary to what some Dinosaurs said at the time, the human heart did not burst on passing the 60 mph barrier; even at 100 mph, ears, limbs and other appendages showed no urge to drop off at the wayside.

Meanwhile the manufacturers have been quietly beavering to increase our sense of comfort and well-being. Now we may sit in ergonomically regulated air-conditioned plushness, listening to our six-speaker stereo, driving with automatic transmission and cruise control, power brakes, power seat adjustment, power windows, power sliding roof . . . What else is there to have? Well, heated seats, for one thing; an automatically dipping mirror, for another, worked by light sensor; automatically dipping headlights . . .

Then there are the voices: for instance, the one that in clipped Anglo-Martian tones reminds you: 'Your door is open . . . your door is open . . . your door is . . .' – until you shut it. 'Please fit your seat belt . . . please fit your seat belt' is another.

These recorded voices are no gimmick, they are here to stay. They in fact symbolize a subtle step forward in car design which has reached the point where the vehicle is now giving orders to the driver. *It* is telling *you* that the door is not closed; *it* is telling *you* to put your seat belt on, that your boot is open, your hand-brake is on.

Will people actually mind the implication that they are becoming slaves to their vehicles? There will be those, the anti-seat belt crowd among them, who will resent such intrusions on their 'privacy' (they always think they are the only people on the road). The manufacturers, for their part, will protest that they are acting in the public interest; by making cars more idiot-proof, they can only help to reduce the accident toll. On balance – just as I favour compulsory wearing of seat belts – I am on the manufacturers' side. Any measure that helps to make one car journey safer must be for the general good.

CITY LIMITS

What, though, can we do for our choked and poisoned cities – and for the urban motorist whose role is to sit chugging for hours amid yellow fumes at traffic lights, giving himself ulcers in the process? Much of the doomsday talk about the future of the car has focused, rightly enough, on the environmental problems that we produce for ourselves, and which surface in the form of paralyzing traffic jams and schizophrenic drivers – charming husbands and fathers, some of them, but slavering frothing monsters when caged inside their car for the daily run to work, and the still more jaded journey home.

Against these familiar portraits of gloom we must set the simple fact that the car remains one of the few truly personal forms of transportation available to us. That is a freedom I think it is worth fighting to preserve. If I want to go somewhere, I don't necessarily want to go on a coach trip; perhaps I don't want to go with the mob. At the same time, personal wants cannot always be paramount. Our cities must breathe if they are to function properly, and the day may come when it will be necessary to set limits, to allow only mass transportation into the inner boxes, the financial, shopping and entertainment quarters. This may take the form of raised monorail or underground train services, linked by pedestrian walkways that will be marvellously freed of the present injunctions to 'Walk/Don't Walk'.

There will be further perks. By then pedestrians will not wish to walk much. They will demand to be carried, on air-conditioned, covered, moving sidewalks, hopping off and on as they please. And so it will probably come to pass. However, as drivers, we shall still want to be able to do our own thing: drive to the mountains or the beach. Go trekking. Go courting in the next generation of Passion Wagons. Visit Auntie.

No, the car will not disappear; only change, as we ourselves must.

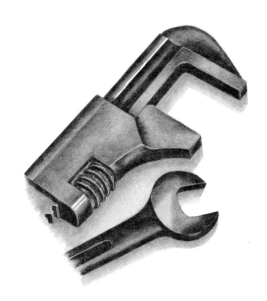